AS TIME WINDS DOWN

To Paul Schlener
Servant of the Living God
      Bud Adamson

> Brace up your minds for action,
> and be alert,
> and fix your hope fully on the
> grace that will be coming to
> you when Jesus Christ is revealed.
>   I Peter 1:13

As Time Winds Down

An Outline of Periods and Events Destined to Close Out the History of the Present World

Bud Adamson

Pleasant Word

© 2008 by Bud Adamson. All rights reserved.

Pleasant Word (a division of WinePress Publishing, PO Box 428, Enumclaw, WA 98022) functions only as book publisher. As such, the ultimate design, content, editorial accuracy, and views expressed or implied in this work are those of the author.

No part of this publication may be reproduced, stored in a retrieval system, or transmitted in any way by any means—electronic, mechanical, photocopy, recording, or otherwise—without the prior permission of the copyright holder, except as provided by USA copyright law.

The author of this book has waived the publisher's suggested editing and proof reading services. As such, the author is responsible for any errors found in this finished product.

Unless otherwise noted, all Scriptures are taken from the *Holy Bible, New International Version®, NIV®*. Copyright © 1973, 1978, 1984 by the International Bible Society. Used by permission of Zondervan. All rights reserved.

Scripture references marked KJV are taken from the King James Version of the Bible.

Scripture references marked NKJV are taken from the New King James Version of the Bible © 1990 by Thomas Nelson, Inc.

Scripture references marked MLB are taken from the Modern Language Bible, The New Berkeley Version in Modern English, Revised Edition © 1969 by Zondervan.

Scripture references marked NEB are taken from the New English Bible © 1970 by University Press of Oxford and Cambridge.

Scripture references marked NET are taken from the NET Bible®, (New English Translation™), © 1996, 1997, 1998, 1999, 2000, 2001 by Biblical Studies Press. All Rights Reserved.

ISBN 13: 978-1-4141-1050-9
ISBN 10: 1-4141-1050-2
Library of Congress Catalog Card Number: 2007904565

Table of Contents

Introduction vii

Period One: The Last Days 13

Period Two: The Day of the Lord 37

Period Three: The Millennial Kingdom 77

Period Four: The Final Conflict 123

Introduction

Jesus Christ Reveals the Chronological Path of Periods and Events Through Time

On the 24th day of the first month, in the year 544 b.c., a man stood alone on the bank of the great Tigress River. After three weeks spent in mourning and fasting, Daniel was waiting for a response from his God, when suddenly he was aware of a visitor. He looked up to behold "a man dressed in linen, his loins girded with fine gold of Ophaz, his body like topaz; his face like lightning; his eyes like flaming torches, his arms and legs like polished bronze, and the sound of his voice like the sound of a multitude" (Dan 10:5,6 MLB).

Though Daniel's companions could not actually see the vision, the apparent nearness of Deity terrified them, and they fled to hiding places. Left alone in the presence of this Glorious Being, Daniel became faint. When his Master actually spoke to him, Daniel was overwhelmed and fell forward unconscious at His feet.

After being revived by the visitor, Daniel was respectfully ordered to rise from his kneeling position and listen intently to the words of his guest. Still trembling greatly, he attempted to obey, but was so overcome with the majesty of the visitor that he could neither raise his head to look upon Him, or open his mouth to answer Him. Then the man-like being touched first Daniel's mouth and then his body, greatly strengthening him, and enabling him to communicate with his guest. Thus prepared, Daniel became the recipient of a special message his Lord had come to deliver to him. A message, Daniel discovered, whose delivery had been delayed 21 days because of the intervention of powerful spiritual foes (Dan 10:13).

Thus began the disclosure of an amazing prophecy, pertaining to a lengthy future struggle involving powerful confederations of nations (Daniel, Chapters 11 and 12). This revelation focused on events and personalities of particular relevance to Daniel's own people, the Jews (Dan 10:14); situations and relationships to be experienced by that nation which would be of dire consequences to them; events destined to take place in Israel's latter history; personalities which this people would meet on earth's stage between the sixth century b.c. and the end of the Day of the Lord.

Centuries later, another man received a lengthy prophetic vision from this very same messenger. While imprisoned on the Isle of Patmos because of his faith and testimony, the Apostle John was also visited by this glorious man-like being, none other than Jesus Christ Himself (Rev 1:1-19). The prophetic vision delivered to John on this latter occasion was directed to all the Lord's servants, "to show them what must shortly take place."

Christ's revelation to John includes some important information concerning the Jewish remnant, but for the most part pertains to the end time experiences of "Many peoples and nations and tongues and kings" (Rev 10:11 KJV). It includes certain events outlined earlier to Daniel, but focuses on the Day of the Lord in much greater detail. In fact, it carries us beyond that period of wrath into the Millennium, and beyond that thousand year kingdom to Judgment, and beyond the Great white Throne into eternal bliss with God the Father, Son and Holy Spirit; encompassing periods, personalities and proceedings far beyond the scope of the message delivered centuries earlier at the River Tigress.

Sandwiched between these two unique revelations to individuals, Christ delivered a discourse to His disciples which also foretold certain events of the last days. On the Mount of Olives, Jesus outlined to His followers the episodes and signs which will precede and introduce His own second coming. Like the other two revelations, all the periods and events which He references are presented in chronological order (Matt 24, Mark 13 and Luke 21).

In His Olivet Discourse, Jesus provides us with a clue as to where and how the events surrounding His coming fit into the prophetic chronology He had delivered to Daniel. The key to such a correlation is a specific event Jesus identified to both Daniel and his disciples, namely the setting up of an abomination in Jerusalem that will result in desolation (Matt 24:15; Dan 11:31, 12:11). Jesus told His disciples that this act would initiate a time of great tribulation for the people of Jerusalem and Judea (Matt 24:15-22). He also informed Daniel of such a period of unprecedented distress to be experienced by his people (Dan 12:1).

Similarly, it is possible to correlate Jesus' Olivet Discourse with His later revelation to John. Both these New Testament accounts of future events include the same unique celestial phenomena first predicted by the Prophet Joel (Joel 2:30, 31). In the Olivet Discourse these cosmic changes are forecast to immediately follow the time of great tribulation and introduce the coming of the Son of Man in power and great glory (Matt 24:29, 30). In Revelation these same celestial signs are also related to an appearance of Christ and predicted to be manifested just prior to the Day of God's Wrath (Rev 6:12-17).

Jesus thus provides us with the keys that make possible a complete correlation of all three of His prophetic chronologies. These Scriptural accounts of God's past, present and future program for mankind may be integrated into a single continuous outline representing a step by step itinerary of selected events from the sixth century b.c. to the very end of time and beyond. Christ has laid out historical stepping stones of personalities, places and proceedings to guide us along this entire journey.

Many of the personalities and events presented in Christ's message to Daniel were associated with the 69 weeks of years which preceded Christ's death and resurrection (Dan 9:25, 26). For purposes of the following study, I have chosen to jump over this ancient history, making the leap from b.c. to a.d., and to begin my outline in the post-resurrection period. It is obvious that prophetic events of this later era are more relevant to the final count down.

The study outline which follows is basically my interpretation of the route revealed by Christ in the three passages of Scripture referenced in preceding paragraphs, a panorama of our final march toward eternity future. I have attempted to weave into His chronology, at appropriate places in the panorama of events, a limited number of supplemental prophetic truths from various portions of His Word. The reader may wish to confirm, complement or correct the basic outline by utilizing it as a depository for filing and organizing additional prophetic facts from throughout the Scriptures.

In the outline I have attempted to identify and properly relate the major events which will consume earth's final years. Many of the details and descriptions necessary for a complete understanding of these prophetic events are not included. Presently, I am leaving it up to the reader to search the Word for this missing data. Eventually, a commentary containing considerable explanatory information will be added to

Introduction

flesh out the skeleton outline. This final portion of the study is presently in the making, and when completed will be of considerable help in clarifying the terminology, interpretations and conclusions presented in the outline.

I have sought the help of the Holy Spirit in my attempt to interpret, correlate and consolidate prophetic facts in a clear and truthful manner. However, it should be recognized that my results represent merely a rough approximation of the path we are upon in our final march to time zero. My hope is that it is at least a close enough approximation to steady our steps and encourage our hearts.

In the outline, we will first focus our attention upon events and personalities associated with the **"last days."** For purposes of this study, I will refer to the last days as Period I, and define it as that period of time which began with Christ's first advent (or His death and resurrection) and will terminate when Christ comes to gather His Church to Himself. The primary focus of this portion of the investigation will be upon those events which we, His servants, may personally witness as we wait for Him.

After we have followed the outline through the age designated as the last days, we will move on to look at those future periods less relevant to our present pilgrimage. Those **"end times"** I have divided into three distinct periods of unequal duration.

The first of these to be previewed will be a seven-year period in which God finally brings the nations into a full accounting of their centuries of iniquity, rejection, and rebellion, and pours out His wrath upon earth's unregenerate masses and their satanic leadership. This abbreviated period of catastrophic judgments I have designated as **Period II**, and identified with the Biblical title, **"The Day of the Lord."** Though God's Day of wrath will not actually reach its conclusion until the very end of time, for purposes of this study I am applying this title to just the initial seven years; a period which will culminate with the **"War of the Sovereign God's Great Day,"** the dreadful transitional conflict to be staged at Armaggeddon.

Period II also corresponds to **Daniel's Seventieth Week**, a future week of years that not only follows the rapture of the Church but also the rebirth of a remnant of Israel, at the time of their hour of greatest trial. During their special week, God will interact with the surviving Jewish elect in unique ways. Confirming His covenant with them for the entire week; the first half on earth, and the second half in heaven.

Christ's victory at Armaggeddon will terminate satanic administration of the earth through sinful men, and usher in the thousand-year reign of Christ which we refer to as **the Millennial Kingdom**. A consideration of that late era of time will constitute the third major division of the outline. That sunset scene will be painted in a different texture. Very little chronology of events will be presented, but instead the portrait of that period will feature the residents of the Millennium; their identity, their relationships with the Lord, their quality of life, their activities, and their purpose will be highlighted against the backdrop of a remarkable landscape and some amazing architecture. The paramount emphasis of that section of the outline will be upon the King Himself, and His objectives for that climatic period of history.

Following the outline and commentary of Period III, a final chapter, presented in a narrative format, will conclude the study. This chapter will be devoted to describing and commenting on the post millennial event that will close out the history of this current world. Though I have referenced this concluding chapter as Period IV, it is so closely related in time and setting to the Millennium that it could almost be considered the final event of Period III. However, it will actually take place immediately after the completion of the 1000 years. At that time, Satan will be released from the Abyss, and the postponed final phase of the Day of the Lord will take place. While the sun and moon still distinguish between day and night, and the clocks tick off earth's final hours, Satan will perpetrate his last delusion of mankind; persuading the unregenerate masses of earth to attack the King and his special people. This rebellion will be an exercise in futility and failure that will be terminated with flame. Following the cremation of earth's armies, and Christ's eternal victory over His archenemy, a second resurrection of the dead occurs. At that time, all those whose names are not written in the Book of Life are judged and condemned to eternal punishment.

Then, as the present heaven and earth are also cremated, all calendars and clocks will cease to exist, and all schedules and appointments rendered obsolete. **Time will have finally wound down, and we will be ready to march into the eternity beyond.**

Period One: The Last Days

I. Period One: The Last Days

From Christ's Provision for the Church to Christ's Coming for the Church

A. **Days Which are Chronicled in Scripture**

   Two separate but parallel chronological revelations of Christ cover this period of time.

   1. The Last Days are the eon (age, era, generation) for which Jesus presented a condensed preview of events in His **OLIVET DISCOURSE** (Matt 24, Mark 13, Luke 21).

   2. The progression of the same major developments within this age are pictured symbolically by the **OPENING OF THE FIRST SIX SEALS** (Rev 6:1-17).

B. **Days Which Commenced With the First Advent, Death and Resurrection of Christ** (Heb 1:1-3, I Pet 1:20).

C. **Days Which Were Confirmed at Pentecost to be Already Underway** (Acts 2:16-18, 21).

   *The Last Days are those in which "WHOSOEVER SHALL CALL ON THE NAME OF THE LORD SHALL BE SAVED." The period in which the Gentile Church will be completed and the Jewish remnant will finally recognize their Messiah. (Rom 11:25, 26).

D. **Days Which Already Confront the Church** (I John 2:18; I Tim 4:1-6)

   We have already witnessed a major portion of the last days.

E. **Days Which Are Clouded by World-Wide Deceit, Divisiveness, Disasters, Destruction and Death- These Events Constitute the First Series of Signs of Christ's Coming.**

   1. **THE RIDER ON THE WHITE HORSE** goes forth (breaking of the **first seal**–Rev 6:1, 2).

      a. This is a period in which counterfeit Messiahs will be common, and deceitful teaching will persist.

b. Christ begins the Olivet Discourse by forewarning the disciples of such deceivers and then repeats this same caution for latter phases of the age.
(1) During the early birth pains (Matt 24:4, 5)
(2) During the period of Apostasy (Matt 24:11)
(3) During the Great Tribulation (Matt 24:23, 24)

Note: It is evident that the Rider on the White Horse continues his conquests throughout and beyond the events depicted by all the riders which follow him.

2. THE RIDERS ON THE RED, BLACK AND PALE HORSES go forth (triggered by the opening of the **second, third, and fourth seals**-Rev 6:3-8). The timing of their ride is synonymous with the period in which **THE EARLY BIRTH PAINS** are experienced (Matt 24:6-8; Luke 21:9-11).

This will be a time of progressive deterioration on earth, fueled by human conflicts and natural catastrophes (contrasting with the supernatural judgments coming from heaven and the Abyss in the Day of the Lord-following the opening of the seventh seal as identified in Part II of this outline).

a. Troubles increasing in intensity and frequency with time as typical of birth pains.

b. Troubles spreading world-wide as the riders continue on their circuits.

c. Troubles expressed in wide-spread warfare, pestilence, plagues, earthquakes, and attacks by predators. Resulting in serious famines, economic chaos, and an extreme mortality rate over at least ¼ of the inhabited earth.

d. Troubles which will continue right up to the time of Christ's coming, but will be compounded by the additional general and specific signs scheduled to occur as the last days progress. The intensified travail resulting from these later events is identified in the sections which follow.

F. Days Which Approach Their Climax With A Period of Unprecedented (1) Rebellion Against God, and (2) Persecution of His Saints.

These developments follow THE OPENING OF THE FIFTH SEAL and Constitute the Second Series of Signs of Christ's Coming.

Note: The account in Rev 6:9-11 of the opening of the fifth seal focuses on the latter of the two actions listed in the preceding heading. However, Jesus, in His discourse, interrelates these two subjects (Matt 24:9-12). I have, therefore, chosen to place them together in the outline of things to occur following the opening of the fifth seal. Severe persecution of God's people will be the natural consequence of Man's extreme enmity against God.

1. A Time of World-Wide Apostasy is experienced: A marked turning away from righteousness, truth, faith and love by the vast majority of mankind (iniquity becomes the accepted protocol of the nations' leaders and peoples).

a. As the last days progress, it will become more and more apparent that a spirit of selfishness, uncontrolled lust, disrespect for others, and rebellion against God has pervaded all society (II Tim 3:1-5).

The Last Days

    b. As the end of this era draws near, the climate of iniquity will intensify and become a full-blown storm of apostasy (II Thess 2:3).

        (1) Uncontrolled Limits: A time when those in rebellion against God go to extremes (eventually leading to the acceptance of Antichrist later in the Day of the Lord-Dan 8:23).

        (2) Spiritual Hypothermia: The chill factor resulting from the strong winds of iniquity will prove lethal to natural affection and love (Matt 24:12).

        (3) Dispensing of Lies: The fog of false teaching will thicken, obscuring the truth and deceiving many (Matt 24:11; I Tim 4:1, 2; II Tim 3:13; 4:3, 4).

        (4) Declaration of Skepticism: Scoffers will add their thunder to the storm, attempting to shake the foundation of God's promises (II Pet 3:3, 4).

2. A Time of Unprecedented Travail for Christians-THE INTERMEDIATE BIRTH PAINS (A title not appearing in the Bible or commonly used, which I have chosen to apply to the experiences of this time).

    a. Hated by the world because of Christ (Matt 24:9; Mark 13:13; Luke 21:17).

    b. Enemies of the State marked for persecution and prosecution (by both religious and civic authorities-Mark 13:9-11; Luke 21:12).

    c. Betrayed by family and friends (Mark 13:12; Luke 21:16).

    d. Some executed (Matt 24:9, Mark 13:12; Luke 21:16).

    e. The parting of the WAY by those without real convictions (The winds of iniquity and the waves of persecution combine to erode the faith of many professing believers).

        (1) Jumping ship (renouncing the faith-Matt 24:10a).

        (2) Joining the enemy (betraying, hating and opposing the faithful-Matt 24:10b).

        (3) Substituting error for truth (escape to alternate and perverted forms of religion-Matt 24:11).

        (4) Throwing in the towel (return to an immoral and selfish life style-Matt 24: 12, 48, 49).

3. A Time of Unprecedented Opportunity for Christians: World-Wide Witness

    a. **God's plan** to reach the entire world with the Gospel prior to Christ's return (Matt 24:14).

    b. **God's purpose** for the persecution of Christians is revealed: unique opportunities to present the Gospel to their opponents (Luke 21:13; Mark 13:9, 10).

    c. **God's presence** remains with them (Mark 13:11). Guaranteed to the very end of the age (Matt 28:20).

    d. **God's power** provides them with an effective defense of their faith and a strong witness to the truth (Luke 21:14, 15; Mark 13:11; Matt 10:19, 20-no need for prepackaging sermons).

    e. **God's perseverance:** His grace and power enable Christians to remain steadfast and gain eternal life (Matt 24:13; Mark 13:13; Luke 21:19).

G. Days Which Contain the Political Rebirth of Israel

1. Before God finally gathers Israel, at the beginning of the Millennium, He will bring them back from the nations for a time of judgment and cleansing. He will purge out the rebels and bring a remnant "into the bond of the covenant (new)." (Ezek 20:33-38). This will be a time when He prepares the remnant for a future permanent citizenship in a restored land (Ezek 20:40-44), but not before He refines them in a trial of unequaled intensity (The subject of Section H which immediately follows).

2. After almost 2,000 years of continuous subjugation by Gentile nations, **Israel became an independent nation again in 1948.** Before and since that time, Jews have returned to their homeland from many parts of the world. God is orchestrating this gathering, just as He will a second (Isa 11:11, 12).

3. Passages which describe conditions and developments during this preliminary sojourn of the Jews, and which seem to harmonize with events we have thus far witnessed in Israel, are found in the writings of the Prophet Zechariah (Zech 10:3-12; 12:1-9).

H. Days Which Will Confront Israel With a Time of Great Tribulation-The Third Series of Signs

1. **The Identification of That Event:**

   a. Foretold: Zech 14:1-5; 12-15; Dan 12:1, 11; Joel 1:6; 2:20, 25.

   b. Described in Olivet Discourse: Matt 24:15-28; Mark 13:14-23; Luke 21:20-24.

   c. Looked back at: Rev 7:14.

2. **The Specificity of That Event:** The time of tribulation is directly related in Scripture to a single event, not a sequel of different end-time events (Matt 24:15-29).

3. **The Character and Intensity of That Event:** A time of unprecedented physical and spiritual misery resulting from a devastating and cruel attack launched upon a land, its people, and its religion (Matt 24:21; Mark 13:19, 20; Dan 12:1). To recognize how truly devastating the attack will be, one must understand the cumulative sufferings this nation has already endured at that time. The attack will be the final and most severe expression of a mighty storm of judgment that has repeatedly swept disabling waves of trouble across this nation for centuries of time (Joel 1:1-7).

4. **The Location of That Event:** Centered in Judea, the focal point of the attack being the City of Jerusalem (Luke 21:20; Matt 24:16; Mark 13:14; Zech 14:2).

5. **The Victims of the Time of Great Misery**

   a. The Primary target of the attack is the Jews (Dan 12:1).

   b. There will likely be world-wide repercussions.
   (1) Jews will be taken away captive into all nations-(Lk 21:24).
   (2) The attacking international army will be destroyed in its entirety (Joel 2:20; Zech 14:3, 12, 13).
   (3) Christians world wide, who are already enduring severe persecution associated with the time of apostasy, may actually experience their greatest opposition during those very days (Rev 7:14). (Not necessarily so. Keep in mind that this is a time when God is dealing primarily with the Jews).

The Last Days

6. **The Scheduled Timing of That Event**

    a. Coming during the period initiated by the **Opening of the Fifth Seal** (Rev 6:9-11).

    Arriving on the heels of the time of apostasy, or more likely concluding that period (a world in rebellion against God first persecutes His Church and then seeks to exterminate His covenant nation).

    b. Immediately preceding the spectacular events which conclude the last days and introduce the coming Lord (Matt 24:29, 30).

    c. Taking place prior to the Day of the Lord. Compare: Joel 1:6-14 with Joel 1:15; Zeph 1:4-13 with Zeph 1:14-18; Rev 6:9-11 with Rev 8:1-19:21. The tribulation period must be distinguished from the period of wrath which begins with the opening of the Seventh Seal.

    d. Occurring at a time when the Gentile Church is already complete and anticipating their very soon gathering (Rom 11:25-26). The Great Tribulation is probably the period during which the remnant Jewish nation is saved-see 9b.

    Note: In accordance with the above timing, the Great Tribulation (Time of extreme misery) will be an introductory event staged in Israel which will very shortly precede the rapture of the Church, as well as the seven year period of wrath which follows.

7. **The Duration of That Period:** A specific confrontation of limited duration (Matt 24:22) in contrast with the magnitude of its intensity.

    Note: that in the Lord's reference to this event, He speaks of a quick response to a single attack; of escaping to short time relief in mountains; of the potential terror of mothers caught in a time of pregnancy or with infants; of the potential arrival of the event during a specific season and a certain day of the week (Matt 24:16-20).

8. **The Actions and Developments Marking That Period:** (Not necessarily listed in sequence of occurrence).

    a. **Possible preliminary events in the Middle East** (See Dan 11:40-45).

    b. **The Attack:** An international army invades the land causing great destruction (Luke 21:20; Joel 1:6-12; Zech 14:2).

    c. **The Abomination That Brings Desolation** (Matt 24:15; Mark 13:14).
       (1) In His Olivet Discourse, Jesus identified **the key sign that would signal the onslaught of the Great Tribulation**. This sign will be the setting up of an abomination in the holy place that would consequently result in desolation. Jesus also noted that this future event would be the very action foretold centuries before by the Prophet Daniel.
       (2) Daniel made two direct references to such a desecration:
           (a) In Daniel 12:11 an abomination resulting in desolation is identified as the starting point of a 1,290 day period of time that would be critical for Israel. I have interpreted the end point of this designated period to be the mid point of the Day of the Lord (See (b) on pg. 52). If this interpretation is correct, the abomination would be standing in the Holy Place just 30 days prior to the beginning of God's period of wrath. This timing would be consistent with that already considered for the Great Tribulation.

(b) In Daniel 11:31 a similar desecrating act is described, but the context of this account would lead us to conclude that the action described relates to a much earlier period of Israel's past history. An abomination resulting in Jerusalem's desolation was placed in God's Temple by the armies of Antiochus Epiphanes in 167 B.C., as part of an attempt to destroy the covenant relationship with God treasured by devote Jews. Though this timing is inconsistent with that of the Great Tribulation, the sequence of the actions taken by the oppressors, and the subsequent resistance, suffering, and purification of the oppressed Jews, appears to be prophetic of Israel's future experiences during their time of great misery (see Dan 11:29-35).

(3) Currently we cannot describe the appearance of this future abomination, but its nature is no secret. An abomination is a life, thought, action, practice or object that is absolutely detestable to God. The term is commonly used in the Bible in reference to idolatry and images used as idols. The references, by both Matthew and Mark, to a "standing" abomination may very well refer to an image of some kind.

(4) The site in which the abomination will stand is identified by Matthew as "the holy place" and Mark as a place "where it does not belong." This "off limits" site is generally considered to be within the Jewish Temple, but if God schedules this event for a time when no temple exists, there are already historical sites that are considered holy by God. In fact, the entire City of Jerusalem, which God has chosen as an earthly dwelling place, is considered His Holy Hill (Dan 9:16; Ex 15:17).

(5) It is possible that this desecrating act will be carried out by a force of hateful enemies prior to the main attack by an international army. The response of the Jews to such sacrilege may actually provoke intervention by an alliance of nations who sympathize with the cause of Israel's enemies. In that case, the setting up of the abomination would be the act that perpetrates and initiates the time of Great Tribulation. An abomination resulting in desolation.

(6) Accompanying the setting up of an abomination will be action to negate the worship of the true God by abolishing ("turning off") the daily sacrifices of the Jews (Dan 12:11). A similar constraint upon the daily sacrifices was forced upon the Jews by the armies of Antiochus, just prior to their desecration of God's temple with an idol statue of the Olympian god Zeus.

Note: In the time of the end, Antichrist will also "take away" the daily sacrifices (Dan 8:11, 12 KJV). However, the word translated "take away" in this latter passage actually means "to be high, i.e. to rise or raise." It may refer to Antichrist's action in stealing worship from the true God by establishing regular worship of himself. If so, this act would represent a devious reversal of the abolishment of sacrifices that will take place during the time of the Great Tribulation.

d. The Casualties:
   (1) Two-thirds of the Jewish population will be killed (Zech 13:8).
   (2) Women in particular will suffer greatly (Zech 14:2; Luke 21:24).
   (3) Half of Jerusalem's residents will be captured and taken into international exile (Zech 14:2; Luke 21:24; Joel 3:2).

e. The Resistance:
   (1) God enters the fight (Zech 14:3).
   (2) "Judah too will fight at Jerusalem" (Zech 14:14).

The Last Days

  (3) The invaders are destroyed (Zech 14:12-15; Joel 2:20).

 f. **The Deliverance** (Dan 12:1).
  (1) A unique escape route is created by the Lord (Zech 14:4).
  (2) The remnant escape to a wilderness retreat after acquiring plenty of provisions from the enemy camps (Zech 14:5, 14; Rev 12:6).
  (3) Their departure is unhurried; guided and guarded by the Lord (Isa 52:12).

 g. **The Aftermath:** Jerusalem begins a period of deterioration under foreign occupants (Luke 21:24).

9. **The Purposes and Ultimate Consequences of the Great Tribulation:** Used by God to remove the final dross from Israel and to purify a remnant for Himself (Zeph 3:11-13).

 a. This period of distress will be the final exercise of God's wrath against the sins of, and the sinners among, this unique nation (Luke 21:22-24). **The dross will be removed** (Ezek 20:33-38; Zeph 1:4-6; 8-13; Zech 13:1-3, 8).

 b. It also will be the period in which the spiritual rebirth of Israel will occur (Rom 11:26). **The Gold will be refined** (Zech 13:1, 9; Dan 12:1, 10; Ezek 20:37; Zeph 3:12, 13).

  (1) The Promises
   (a) Israel will return to the Lord in the latter days (Deut 4:30, 31; Hosea 3:5).
   (b) Jacob will be saved in a time of trouble (Jer 30:7).
   (c) A remnant will be preserved and gathered during a time of affliction (Isa 10:21-23; 17:4-6; Dan 12:1).
   (d) The entire nation will experience a sudden spiritual rebirth (Isa 66:6-8).
   (e) The remnant will be made righteous (Zeph 3:12, 13).
   (f) All Israel will be saved following the completion of the Gentile Church (Rom 11:25, 26).

  (2) The Enactment: God will prepare many hearts to recognize Christ and exercise true repentance (Zech 12:10-14; Joel 2:12-17; Hosea 5:15-6:3; Zeph 3:9).

  (3) The Fulfillment
   (a) Pity and provision for forgiveness is extended by God to the entire nation of survivors (Zech 13:1; Joel 2:18).
   (b) This remnant are refined as a result of their time of testing (Zech 13:9).
   (c) Consequently a unique relationship is established between the survivors and their God (Zech 13:9).
   (d) This renewal is the deliverance on Mt. Zion promised to the Prophet Joel. The Jewish remnant are the last ones to be included in God's promise: "Whosoever shall call on the name of the Lord shall be delivered." (Joel 2:32 KJV).
   (e) God will then intervene in the conflict to physically deliver at least half of the remnant from their enemies (Zech 14:2-5, Matt 24:22). The cheer will then go up: "Blessed is He who comes in the name of the Lord." (Matt 23:39) (An additional passage which possibly references this deliverance is Isa 52:8-12).

  Note: This deliverance is the escape identified previously in Section 8f, at the top of this page. The confirmation of this escape, and the subsequent protection of the remnant in a wilderness refuge, will be covered in Part II of the outline.

(f) It is very likely that even the 1/2 of the Jewish survivors who are carried into captivity throughout the earth [Refer back to d(3) on pg 18] will be spiritually saved. Either at the same time as their brethren who escape, or during their captivity (Deut 4:27-31). The Prophets repeatedly tell of Jews scattered among the nations who are scheduled to be re-gathered and return to the land at the beginning of the Millennium (see PERIOD III). If they are faithful to the Lord, during the reign of Antichrist, they will be among the martyrs who will be resurrected to reign with Christ (Rev 20:4). In the meantime, the Lord takes their spirits to a safe haven, where for a short time they will wait out the judgments He will inflict upon the world during the Day of the Lord. At the conclusion of that period of wrath, they will exit the waiting room to enter the joyful state of being a very special part of His Millennial Kingdom (Isa 26:19-27:3, 6).

c. The Great Tribulation appears to fulfill a three fold forecast of Israel's future status as presented in Isaiah 40:2: (1) She has received from the Lord's hand double for her sins; (2) Her iniquity is pardoned; (3) Her warfare is completed.

I. **Days Which Reach Their Conclusion With Two Final Signs-This Fourth Series of Signs are Scheduled to Appear Following THE OPENING OF THE SIXTH SEAL.** Though quite different in nature, these final two signs will be so closely linked in a time sequence that they will merge to form a single grand fall of the curtain on the last days.

1. **Sign #1: Special Celestial and Terrestrial Transformations of Universal Proportions.**

    a. **First forecast by the Prophet Joel** (Joel 2:31, 32).
    (1) He described dramatic celestial transformations: "The sun shall be changed into darkness; and the moon into blood..."
    (2) He also noted terrestrial phenomena: "blood, fire and smoke."
    (3) He predicted that this compound mega sign would precede the arrival of "the dark and terrible Day of the Lord."
    (4) He predicted that these physical transformations would follow a series of spiritual manifestations, all occurring within a period when **"Whosoever shall call on the name of the Lord shall be saved."**
    (5) He closely associated these signs with a time in which God would call to Himself and save a remnant of Jews.

    b. **Referenced by other O.T. Prophets** (Isa 13:9, 10; 34:4, Zech 14:6, 7).

    c. **Forecast also by Christ** (Matt 24:29; Luke 21:25, 26).
    (1) To immediately follow the Great Tribulation.
    (2) To include solar changes: Darkening of the sun; failure of the moon to shed its normal light.
    (3) To also involve other celestial bodies: The falling of the stars as the forces in heaven are shaken [see notes on e(2),(c),and(d), page 21].
    (4) To be accompanied by distress on the earth: Specific events to include the roaring of sea and waves [see note on e(3), page 21].
    (5) To immediately precede the Sign of the Son of Man (the 2nd sign of the final sequence).

    d. **Referenced by the Apostle Peter on the Day of Pentecost** (Acts 2:16-21).
    (1) Peter quotes Joel's description of the celestial and terrestrial transformations.

The Last Days

- **(2)** He recognizes that these phenomenon will occur as a sequel to earlier last day signs of a spiritual nature which actually began to be fulfilled on that very day.
- **(3)** He again identifies them as events which precede The Day of the Lord.
- **(4)** He again associates them with a period in which "Whosoever shall call on the Lord will be saved." Could the outpouring of the Holy Spirit represent the beginning of that period of grace, and the celestial and terrestrial signs the end?
- **(5)** Peter omits the portion of Joel's prophecy announcing the delivery of a remnant in Mt. Zion and Jerusalem. Evidently that phase of salvation by grace was not initiated on The Day of Pentecost but must be delayed until the Gentile Church is complete (Rom 11:25).

e. Actually Seen by the Apostle John in a Vision (Rev 6:12-14).
- **(1)** Revealed at THE OPENING OF THE SIXTH SEAL.
- **(2)** Included celestial transformations:
  - **(a)** Sun turned as black as sackcloth.
  - **(b)** Full moon became like blood.
  - **(c)** Stars of heaven fell toward earth.

  Note: Even traveling at the speed of light, these stars would not reach earth for millions of years. They will hardly have begun their journey when, approximately 1,007 years later, God will destroy both the stars and the target, creating a new heaven and a new earth.

  - **(d)** Sky retreated in such a way as to give the appearance of a scroll being rolled up.

  Note: The stars will fall vertically toward the earth. However, to an observer on the earth, over a great length of time, the stars would appear to converge into a more congested pattern; like a scroll being rolled up. Since God will alter the powers of the heavens, this convergence could possibly occur at an accelerated rate. In order for this descent of the stars to be visible on earth precisely at God's appointed time, He would have ordered them on their way millenniums ago.

- **(3)** Accompanied by terrestrial transformations: A tremendous earthquake which dislodges every mountain and island.

  Note: An earthquake of such magnitude could very well be triggered by the celestial transformation we have already noted. Likewise, the tossing of the sea, described by Jesus, would result from the altering of the tides as influenced by changes to the sun and moon. Ocean turbulence and tidal waves would be further magnified by the earthquake itself. A quake that moved mountains and islands would most certainly result in catastrophic damage on both sea and land. Innumerable and uncontrollable fires will be triggered, resulting in tremendous loss of life. Such results are summarized by the Prophet Joel: "Blood, fire and smoke." Thus we note that all the various Scriptural accounts of this complex event, though looking at it from somewhat different perspectives, are quite harmonious in their reports of its magnitude and assessment of its damage. Each revelation seems to supply some additional details.

- **(4)** This compound sign will immediately precede a time in which earth's residents will see a manifestation of the Father and Son, as evidenced by their subsequent reaction. (Rev 6:15-17; Luke 21:26, 27). They will realize at that point that the Day of God's wrath is upon them, and the helplessness of their desperate position. (See also Isa 2:12, 19).

f. **According to the foregoing predictions, the future manifestations of this special compound sign will result in A SHAKING OF BOTH HEAVEN AND EARTH.**
   (1) Such a dual catastrophe is foretold by several of the Prophets (Hag 2:6, 21; Isa 13:13; Joel 3:16).
   (2) The manifestation of this universal shaking seems to be scheduled for a time just preceding or at the beginning of the Day of the Lord, and associated in context with the darkening of sun and moon (Isa 13:13; Joel 3:14-16).
   (3) The shaking of heaven and earth is the sign that marks the entrance to an era of hopelessness (Isa 2:19-21), but is to be preceded by a time in which men still have the opportunity to heed God and be saved by faith (Heb 12:24-27). These facts are consistent with what we already have learned about the last days.
   (4) **God will terminate the final three eras of present world history with gigantic international earthquakes** whose source fault seems to pass through the very center of the earth. The first one, scheduled for the end of the last days, is the one we have just identified as a sign preceding Christ's coming. The second will be activated at the end of the Day of the Lord and will be the greatest of all time (Rev 16:18). The third will be triggered at the end of the Millennium (Ezek 38:19, 20). Only the first seems to be directly associated with a joint shaking of both celestial bodies and the earth.

g. **Explanation:** The reason so much attention has been given to this compound sign is to emphasize its important role in prophetic interpretation. **It is a benchmark in God's prophetic program, appearing on the very border between eras. It marks the exit from the last days and the doormat at the entrance to the Day of the Lord. It immediately follows the Great Tribulation and immediately precedes the Second Coming of Christ. It has implications to both the Church and the Jewish remnant.** God has seen fit to make it a special key for unlocking prophesy by referring to it in a number of different contexts, including two of Christ's chronologies of end time events.

The shaking of heaven and earth catches the attention of human residents of earth for sure! "THEN," as they look skyward, they behold another sign which immediately follows, and which brings them either even greater consternation or unspeakable joy. Against the backdrop of the darkness produced when the solar system lights will be extinguished, an indescribable spectacle of brilliance will appear!

2. **Sign #2: THE APPEARANCE OF THE LORD JESUS CHRIST** (Matt 24:27; Rev 1:7).

   a. **The Sign** of the Son of Man appears in the sky (Matt 24:30).

   b. **The Savior** Himself is seen descending from heaven (Matt 24:30; Mark 13:26, Luke 21:27; I Thess 4:17; Rev 6:16).

   Note: The Sign of the Son of Man and His personal appearance may be synonymous. Matthew prefaces His description of Christ's appearance with the announcement of a sign, but Mark and Luke, in their accounts of this same event, focus immediately on the appearance of Christ "in the clouds with great power and glory" (identical to Matthews description), and make no mention of a preliminary sign. The sign of His coming probably refers to the glory of God that will clothe Christ (Matt 16:27, 24:27; II Thess 1:7). Signs are wonders given to provide authenticity. The glory, which will be revealed at Christ's coming will be of such quality and intensity that none will question its source or who He is. Men will very quickly identify Him

The Last Days

as the Lamb of God and associate Him with the One who sits on the throne (Rev 6:16). In fact He will appear sitting on the right hand of the Father (Mark 14:62).

c. **The Setting:** "On the clouds of heaven"
   (1) As foretold to His enemies (Mark 14:62).
   (2) As foretold to His disciples (Acts 1:9-11).

   Note: Most of the Last Days are included in the period between Christ's departure on the clouds and His coming again on the clouds (Acts 1:11).

d. **The Show:** "with great power and glory" (Matt 16:27; 24:27, 30; Mark 8:38; 13:26; Luke 17:22-24; 21:27; I Thess 4:16; II Thess 1:7; Titus 2:13).
   (1) One of the words rendered "coming" in English translations, and always related to Christ's next visible manifestation to His Church, is "Epiphaneia" which means "a shining forth" (I Tim 6:14; II Tim 4:1, 8; Titus 2:13).
   (2) When Christ informed His disciples of the spectacular glory associated with His coming, He noted just two things that must transpire prior to this appearance: (a) His suffering on behalf of mankind, and (b) His rejection by mankind (Lk 17:22-25). Both of these actions occurred at His first coming. Therefore, His very next appearance will be the spectacular event He forecast. This will be His arrival in the clouds to gather the Church to Himself.
   (3) The disciples were informed that the authenticity of Christ's return would be confirmed by the awesome display of glory that would accompany it (Matt 24:25-27).

e. **The Sound:** "With a shout, with the voice of the archangel, and with the trump of God" (I Thess 4:16 KJV; Matt 24:31)

f. **The Sight:** "Every eye shall see Him"–no secret appearance (Rev 1:7).
   (1) Recognized as the **"Son of Man"** (Matt 24:30).

   Note: Jesus told the high priest who was interrogating Him at His trial: "You will see the **Son of Man** seated at the right hand of the Almighty, coming on the clouds of heaven" (Mk 14:62).

   (2) Recognized as **"The Lamb"** (Rev 6:16).

   Note: Men of the world, who know nothing of Christ, do not naturally or spontaneously think of Him as the Lamb of God. On this occasion they must actually view Him as the glorified Lamb of God, seated next to the enthroned glory of the Father. This is not the image of Christ that men will see at His latter appearance at Armageddon (Rev 19:11-16).

   (3) His relationship to humanity (**Son of Man**) and His redemptive work (**Lamb of God**) are the characteristics of Christ most readily recognized by observers at the initial appearance of His second coming. In a later appearance of this same "parousia" (arrival and continued presence), the names and titles used to describe Him will magnify His Deity: "**Faithful and True**," "**Word of God**," "**King of Kings** and **Lord of Lords**." Initially he comes to execute the final bodily redemption of believers He died for and to take His church to Heaven. At the end of the day of the Lord, He comes to execute His sovereign wrath against those who have rejected Him, and to establish His Kingdom upon the earth. The appearance we are discussing at this point in our outline is the former.

g. **The Sorrow:** The reaction of most of earth's inhabitants to His coming:
   (1) Surprise

- **(a)** The status quo prevails (Matt 24:37-39; Lk 17:26-29).
- **(b)** People are involved in their normal occupations (Matt 24:40, 41).
- **(c)** Peace and safety prevail–their guard is down (I Thess 5:2, 3).

Note: Christ's latter appearance at Armageddon will not be unexpected but rather anticipated. The Beast, and an army mustered well in advance from throughout the earth, will assemble to actually await Christ's attack, intent on repelling it and realizing a victory over the Prince of princes (Rev 19:19; 16:13-16; Dan 8:25).

- **(2)** Terror (Rev 6:15-17; Isa 2:19-22).
- **(3)** Grief (Matt 24:30; Rev 1:7).

Note: World-wide recognition of Christ seems to be almost immediate, followed by deep conviction and fear, but not repentance and faith. The time in which "Whosoever shall call on the name of the Lord shall be saved" has been terminated. Opportunity for salvation is gone. Their grieving is not godly sorry that results in repentance, but rather the sorrow of the world that results in death (2 Cor 7:10).

h. The Schedule:
- **(1)** The exact timing of His arrival is known only to the Father (Matt 24:36).
- **(2)** Preliminary signs will alert us to the approach of "that day." The coming of Christ is the focal point of the entire Olivet Discourse. Everything He taught His disciples on that occasion pointed toward His coming; both the course of world history He unveiled, and the specific signs He identified.
  - **(a)** He will not appear before all the signs are displayed (Matt 24:33-35).
  - **(b)** The signs announcing His coming are to be observed and interpreted (Matt 24:32-33).
  - **(c)** We cannot accurately or correctly estimate the exact time of His coming, but we can increase both our perception of its approximate nearness, and our readiness for its arrival. This is accomplished through a life of expectancy; one that demonstrates faithfulness and love (Matt 24:42-46; I John 2:28).
  - **(d)** We can see the Day of Christ approaching clearly enough to motivate us to encourage other believers (Heb 10:25).
  - **(e)** When believers still resident on earth see the latter of the signs displayed, they may be assured that He is at the very door (Matt 24:32-33).
  - **(f)** His coming should take no Christians by surprise (I Thess 5:4-6). Such alertness is contrasted with the surprise of the unsaved (I Thess 5:2-3).

J. Days Which Culminate When Christ Gathers His Saints To Himself–The rapture of the Church. (The last days began with the completion of Christ's gospel work and will end with the completion of His Church.)

1. The initial purpose of His coming back
   - **a.** To take us to Himself (John 14:3).
   - **b.** To rescue us from the wrath to come (I Thess 1:10, 5:9).

2. The accomplishment of this purpose will be achieved through **a bodily RESURRECTION** of both dead and living believers.

The Last Days

  a. **The Promise:** Resurrection is for all who belong to Him (I Cor 15:20-23).
  b. **The Product:** A completely changed body (I Cor 15:51-52).
      (1) From mortality to immortality (I Cor 15:53-54).
      (2) From perishable to imperishable (I Cor 15:42, 53-54).
      (3) From dishonor to glory (I Cor 15:43).
      (4) From weakness to power (I Cor 15:43).
      (5) From a natural body to a spiritual (I Cor 15:44).
      (6) From a vile body to a glorious body resembling Christ's (Rom 8:29; I Cor 15:49; Phil 3:20-21; I John 3:2).
  c. **The Signal:** Resurrection occurs at the sound of the last trumpet blast of the last days (I Cor 15:52; I Thess 4:16; Matt 24:31). This will be the last sound to signal deliverance before the Day of the Lord begins and the trumpets only signal God's judgments.

  Note: This is not the last resurrection to life with Christ. There will be later phases of this first resurrection, which will occur within approximately 7+ years of this trumpet blast (Rev 14:1-4, 20:4-6).

  d. **The Length of Time for the Transformation to Take Place:** "In a flash, in the twinkling of an eye" (I Cor 15:52).
  e. **The Order:** Christians who have already died physically will precede those who remain alive to the hour of His coming (I Thess 4:15-17).

3. **THE GATHERING**—the last order of business of the last days (Matt 24:31).
  a. **The Gatherers:** Angels are sent out by Christ to gather His elect (the Church).
      (1) They are dispatched with a loud trumpet call. Probably the same trumpet call that dispatches the angels earthward is the one that calls the church heavenward (2c above).
      (2) This assignment given the angels contrasts greatly with the responsibility given a single angel when the Lord later rides to victory at Armageddon (Rev 19:17-18).
      (3) The Bible clearly predicts a future gathering of that portion of Israel's elect that have been scattered among the nations. This will take place at the beginning of the Millennium, but it will not be carried out by angels. The remnant will actually be escorted and served by delegates of the very lands that had enslaved them (Isa 14:2, 49:22-23). Their journey back will be over earth's surface and not through the heavens (Isa 66:20). The Lord will be awaiting them in Jerusalem and not in the clouds (Ezek 34:13-16).
      (4) There will be another harvest undertaken by angels. At His second coming they will concentrate on gathering the good grain but at the end of His earthly reign they will reap the weeds (Matt 13:39-42).
  b. **The Field:** The elect are to be gathered "from the four winds. From one end of the heavens to the other" (Matt 24:31). Let's consider a possible scenario: Christians distributed horizontally throughout the entire earth will be raised vertically into the atmosphere over their former place of residence or burial. There, scattered throughout earth's enveloping atmosphere, they will be gathered by the angels and brought to Christ. According to Mark's account of Christ's description, His chosen will be gathered "from the ends of the earth to the end of the heavens" (Mark 13:27).

- c. **The Condition of the Grain:**
  - **(1)** Kept for that day (I Cor 1:8-9; Phil 1:6-10).
  - **(2)** Transformed during harvest (Described in J2b on the preceding page)
- d. **The Destination of the Harvest:** "To Meet the Lord in the Air" (I Thess 4:17).
- e. **The Future of the Reaped Grain:** "Ever be with the Lord" (I Thess 4:17 KJV)
  - **(1)** Witnessing His Glory (John 17:24).
  - **(2)** Enjoying His presence, protection, and guidance (Rev 7:15-17; 21:3; 22:4)
  - **(3)** Clothed with His righteousness (2 Tim 4:8; Rev 7:14; 19:8).
  - **(4)** Recipients of the incomparable riches of His grace (Eph 2:7).
  - **(5)** Joint heirs with Christ of an inheritance that is imperishable, undefiled, and unfading (I Peter 1:4-5; Rom 8:17).
  - **(6)** Serving Him (Rev 7:15; 22:3).

K. Days Conducted in Watchfulness: (Matt 24:42-44)

1. **The Focus of the Watchman:** Christ's purpose in disclosing His latter day's agenda is to focus our attention on **HIS SECOND COMING.** The progressive degradations and dangers of a sin cursed world, as well as the more specific signs, are all presented as stepping stones which lead us ever closer to the day of deliverance and glory (Matt 24:6-13). **THE SIGNS ALL LEAD TO THE SAVIOR.**

2. **The Path of the Watchman:** Christ unveils the dark realities of the present age in order to prepare us for rough times (Matt 24:9; Mk 13:12-13), to warn us of impending dangers (Mk 13:21-23; Matt 24:48-51), to define our opportunities (Mk 13:9; Lk 21:13-15), to clarify the scope of our responsibility (Matt 24:14; Mk 13:10), and to expose our limitations (Matt 24:42).

3. **The Role of the Watchman:** Assuring us of our union with Him at His glorious coming (Mk 13:26-27), and of His present role in our lives through the Holy Spirit (Mk 13:11), He challenges us to a life of expectancy (Mk 13:29), alertness (Mk 13:33-37), courage (Mk 13:7, 11), discipline (Lk 21:34), stability in doctrine (Matt 24:23-27), faithfulness in service (Matt 24:45-47; 25:15, 19, 29), prayer (Lk 21:36), and steadfastness (Mk 13:13; Lk 21:19).

WATCHING FOR CHRIST IS FOREMOST EXPRESSED IN LIVING FOR HIM AND LIKE HIM!

4. **The Development of the Watchman:**

WHILE THE HEADLINE OF CHRIST'S OLIVET DISCOURSE IS HIS COMING, THE BOTTOM LINE IS A LIFE THAT IS UNASHAMED BEFORE HIM AT HIS COMING (Matt 24:46; I Jn 2:28).

The countdown until His coming is intended to be a time of purification (Tit 2:12-13), in which both our hope (I Jn 3:2-3; Phil 3:20-21), and our investments (I Cor 15:51-58; Dan 12:3), are placed in the eternal; a time when our character prepares us to face "that day" with confidence (I Jn 4:17), and our fruit enables us to realize the fullness of its joys (Matt 25:21; I Thess 2:19-20).

# The Last Days

5. **The Handbook of the Watchman:** The preceding comments relating to watchfulness are based primarily on the words of Jesus as presented in the Olivet Discourse. This section of Scripture is a gold mine full of nuggets of encouragement and instruction for Christians enduring the birth pains while awaiting the coming of the Lord. Unfortunately, it is commonly taught that this discourse is instead a second hand shop (i.e. that the instruction given therein to believers is really directed to a group other than the Church; Chosen ones who will occupy earth's stage after the Church has been raptured). Therefore, the truths disclosed by Christ are not considered directly applicable to you and I. In section L which follows, are listed some of the reasons why I believe Christ was describing events and circumstances of the last days and not the Day of the Lord. Consequently, I believe the revelations and instructions provided by the Lord were directed to the Church, and are literally and directly applicable to you and I. The agents through whom He conveyed these truths were the Apostles, the very ones who still form an integral part of the foundation upon which the entire Church is constructed (Eph 2:20). Over a dozen times in His address the Lord relates His teaching to His apostles by use of the personal pronoun "you."

In their quest for personal discernment, the disciples had asked Christ some rather specific questions related to His coming and the identity of the signs which would precede His arrival. The Lord not only provided some satisfactory answers, but supplemented His response with instructions guiding their own response to the forthcoming events. It is quite obvious that He speaks of situations and actions which He expects His followers (later called Christians) to experience: "**You** will hear," "**You** will be handed over," "**You** will be hated," "so when **you** see," "**your** flight," "if anyone says to **you**," "see I have told **you** ahead of time," "if anyone tells **you**," "when **you** see these things," "**you** do not know what day **your** Lord will come," "**you** also must be ready!"

It is interesting to note that a good part of the warnings, challenges, and personal instructions given by Jesus in the Olivet Discourse were reiterations or echoes of similar instruction given to the disciples on other occasions. In fact many of them are repeated almost verbatim. When we inspect these instructions in their original context, we discover that without exception, they were directed to the Lord's disciples. This fact would seem to reinforce the internal evidence, in the text of the discourse itself, that Christ's teaching on the Mount of Olives was indeed given for the benefit of His followers, and through them the Church. The words of wisdom given on that occasion were designed to guide us as we currently wait, watch, and work.

During His final week in the flesh, Jesus again communicated to His disciples some of His prior directives. He made them even more meaningful by placing them into the context of His coming for the Church.

The following table identifies some of the truths echoed by Jesus in the Olivet Discourse, which were also included in prior instructions from the Lord **to His disciples**. Cross-references are given to pinpoint the occasion of the earlier teaching and to verify the identity of the intended audience.

	Olivet Discourse	Subject	Communicated on another occasion	Party Addressed
a.	Matt 24:9; Mk 13:13; Lk 21:12	Worldwide hatred and persecution **because of Christ**.	Matt 10:22	Matt 10:1
b.	Mk 13:9; Lk 21:12	Arrest and imprisonment on account of Christ, will lead to opportunities to testify on His behalf.	Matt 10:17-18	Matt 10:1
c.	Mk 13:11; Lk 21:14-15	**How to be unprepared** for interrogation and trial.	Matt 10:19-20; Lk 12:11-12	Lk 12:1,4,8
d.	Mk 13:12; Lk 21:16	Betrayal by family members.	Matt 10:21,34-36	Matt 10:1
e.	Mk 13:12; Lk 21:16	Some will be killed.	Jn 16:2	Jn 13:1; 16:1
f.	Matt 24:13; Mk 13:13; Lk 21:19	Steadfastness in the face of persecution will be rewarded.	Matt 10:22; Rev 2:10	Matt 10:1
g.	Lk 21:18	The hairs of your head numbered (in both contexts relates to God's care during persecution).	Matt 10:30	Matt 10:1
h.	Matt 24:17-18; Mk 13:14-16	Let go of worldly possessions and flee judgment.	Lk 17:30-32	Lk 17:22

Note: In the Olivet Discourse Jesus relates this instruction to believers in Judea during Israel's time of great tribulation. In Lk 17 it would seem that Jesus is relating this same instruction to believers at Christ's return and to the impending judgment of the Day of the Lord. For emphasis He adds, "Remember Lot's wife!" The rapture will almost immediately follow the tribulation period. Luke directs His instruction in Lk 17:30-32 to Gentile believers who are not likely to be in Judea during the tribulation period, but whose response to Christ's coming is to be similar to that of obedient Jewish believers residing in Judea during Israel's hour of great anxiety.

i.	Matt 24:23-26 Mk 13:21-23	Caution against false announcements of Christ's coming.	Lk 17:23	Lk 17:22
j.	Matt 24:27	His coming will be unmistakably glorious.	Lk 17:24	Lk 17:22
k.	Matt 24:28	Christians will be gathered to where the object of their affections and source of their life (Christ) is located.	Lk 17:37	Lk 17:22

The Last Days

	Olivet Discourse	Subject	Communicated on another occasion	Party Addressed
l.	Matt 24:36 Mk 13:32	The timing of His coming is known only to the Father.	Acts 1:6-7 [a later disclosure by Jesus rather than a prior one.]	Acts 1:2,6
m.	Matt 24:38-39	The similarity between events and attitudes preceding and accompanying Christ's coming, and those accompanying the deliverance from judgment of Noah and Lot. (The rapture will also be a deliverance from judgment because it immediately precedes the Day of the Lord—It will be the busiest day of travel in the history of the earth as every soul rushes to a destination. Those whose names are written in the Lamb's book of life to the Lord, and everyone else into the Day of the Lord.)	Lk 17:26-30	Lk 17:22
n.	Matt 24:42,44,50 Mk 13:33 Lk 21:34	An unexpected return.	Lk 12:40	Lk 12:22,32
o.	Matt 24:42-44 Mk 13:33-37 Lk 21:34-36	Alertness while awaiting His return.	Lk 12:35-40	Lk 12:22,32
p	Matt 24:45-47	Faithfulness while awaiting His return.	Lk 12:42-44	Lk 12:22,32
q.	Matt 24:48-51	Unfaithfulness will be punished.	Lk 12:45-46	Lk 12:22,32
r.	Matt 24:40-41	The gathering.	Lk 17:34-36	Lk 17:22

Note: Luke's gospel was directed to Gentile believers. If Jesus was describing a re-gathering of Israel, He probably would not have included it in Luke's account. The exit described in this passage is given in the context of a challenge to the disciples to forsake this world's values in order to gain eternal rewards, to lose their life in order to find it. The rapture will conclusively verify the wisdom of having an eternal sense of values.

L. Days Which Contrast with the Seven Year Period Preceding Christ's Later Appearance at Armageddon (Contrasting the Last Days with the Day of the Lord).

1. Days characterized by natural catastrophes (Matt 24:7, 8). Contrasted with days of supernatural catastrophes (Rev 8:6-9:20, 16:1-21).

   Note: None of the signs of Christ's coming which He previewed in His discourse with the disciples are included in the account of events to take place in the Day of the Lord (Rev 8-19). On the other hand, none of the gigantic, catastrophic judgments that will precede Christ's appearance on the white charger (The War of the Sovereign God's Great Day), are even mentioned by Christ in the Olivet Discourse.

2. Days which include multinational conflicts (Matt 24:6-7). Contrasted with the first half of the day of the Lord when the nations are under attack by supernatural armies (Rev 9), and the second half of the Day of the Lord when a single world dictator controls all the nations and their military forces (Rev 13:2, 4, 7; 17:12-13; 16:13-14).

3. Days in which false prophets will claim to be Christ (Matt 24:5, 11, 24). Contrasted with a time in which a single false prophet will deify the Beast (Rev 13:11-17).

   Note: Neither the Beast nor Satan, two of the chief personalities on the earth during the Day of the Lord, are mentioned, or even eluded to, in Christ's Olivet Discourse.

4. Days of persecution of Christians on the earth (Matt 24:9). Contrasted with days in which the Church is in heaven enjoying the Lord (Rev 7:9, 10, 13-17), and participating in the marriage feast of the Lamb (Rev 19:6-9).

5. Days in which Satan pursues Christians (I Pet 5:8-9). Contrasted with days in which He pursues the Jewish remnant (Rev 12:13-17).

6. Days in which the gospel is being preached throughout the entire earth by resident Christians (Matt 24:14). Contrasted with days in which the only preaching is conducted by two special witnesses in Jerusalem (Rev 11:3-6), and by a single angel (Rev 14:6, 7).

7. Days in which the Jews reside in Jerusalem and Judea (Lk 21:20-22). Contrasted with days in which they reside in a wilderness retreat (Rev 12:6, 14).

8. Days in which Jerusalem will be surrounded, overrun, and destroyed (Lk 21:20-24; Zech 14:2). Contrasted with days in which Mystery Babylon will be destroyed (Rev 14:8; 16:19; 17:16-18; 18:2-24).

9. Days in which the majority of Jews suffer defeat and death as a judgment for sin (Lk 21:22-24; Zech 13:8). Contrasted with days in which a holy remnant of Jews (survivors) are defeated by the Antichrist (Rev 13:7).

10. Days which conclude with men, including military leaders, scattered upon the mountains attempting to hide from God in anticipation of the beginning of the Day of His wrath (Rev 6:15-17). Contrasted with days, which conclude with men assembled by the military leaders in a mighty army on

The Last Days

the mountains of Israel, intent on fighting the Lord, on the very eve of the culmination of His Day of Wrath (Rev 19:19-21). **Unsaved men will mourn at Christ's first appearance of His second coming** (Matt 24:30). **They will curse God prior to His final appearance** (Rev 16:9, 11, 21).

11. Days of status quo as the end is approached (Matt 24:37-41). Contrasted with days of complete chaos, anxiety, and upheaval as the end is approached (Rev 16:1-21). At the end of the Day of the Lord, nothing will be happening as usual or in a normal fashion.

12. Days of unexpectedness by the unregenerate, as the time of His coming draws near (Matt 24:38-39; Lk 21:34-35). Contrasted with days of expectancy and preparations by the unregenerate for His arrival (Rev 16:14; 19:19).

13. Days which approach their conclusion with believers still awaiting on the earth (Matt 24:33). Contrasted with days that terminate with only the rebellious resident on the earth (Rev 16:9, 11, 21), all resurrected believers assembled in His heavenly cavalry (Rev 19:14). **In one case, the Church is ready to exit earth, in the other case it is ready to return to it.** As the signs preceding His initial coming are witnessed, believers are told to **"lift up your heads"** in anticipation of your redemption (Lk 21:28). At the final appearance of His second coming, the only believers still resident on the earth are **beheaded**, and in graves awaiting their resurrection (Rev 20:4).

14. Days which conclude with a host of angels escorting the Church to the Lord who awaits them "on the clouds of the sky" (Matt 24:31). Contrasted with days, following the conclusion of the Day of the Lord, when Israel's former gentile captors will escort a remnant of that nation overland to the Lord who awaits them in Jerusalem (Isa 49:22, 23).

15. Days which end with men on earth anticipating the outpouring of God's wrath (Rev 6:16, 17), and about to witness the destruction of the earth and its occupants (Rev 11:18; Isa 13:9). Contrasted with days whose termination marks the beginning of an era when men on earth will benefit from God's righteous reign, and witness the miraculous reconstruction of portions of the earth (Isa 51:3; Psa 48:1, 2), and the salvation of many of its inhabitants (Psa 98:2-9; 87:4).

I-II Twilight: Moving From One Age To Another

The Abrupt Transition From The Last Days Into The Day Of The Lord

A. Sunset will be Very Closely Followed by Darkness

1. The night is coming (Jn 9:4; Joel 2:1-2; Amos 5:18, 20; Zeph 1:15). (This night is the subject of Period II).

2. Just before spiritual darkness falls, a brilliant sunset will illuminate the earth: The glory of Christ's coming (Already described as the concluding event of the Last days–refer to "The Show" on page 23).

3. **When Christ is revealed in the clouds, two climatic events will take place in rapid succession: The glorification of the Church and the initiation of judgment against those who reject Him (II Thess 1:6-10).**

    a. Christians are to look forward to both His coming (Tit 2:13) and the Day of the Lord (II Pet 3:12); the two arriving essentially on the same day, but separated just enough that we will not experience the latter.

    Note: We have the opportunity to participate with God in bringing that day to a timely reality by contributing to the program He will fulfill prior to its revelation (II Pet 3:11-12).

    b. Both of these events will arrive as a thief in the night (same thief, same night).
    (1) Christ's appearance (Matt 24:42-44).
    (2) Day of the Lord (II Pet 3:10; I Thess 5:2-3)–note that this day is directly related in the context of this latter passage to the rapture (I Thess 4:16-17), and to the anticipation of His return by Christians (I Thess 5:4-9).

    c. Both of these events will be preceded by the same sign:
    (1) Christ's appearance (Matt 24:29-31).
    (2) Day of the Lord (Rev 6:12-17).
    At approximately the same time that Christians anticipate meeting Christ in heaven's clouds, there will be miserable expectations on earth's surface.

    d. At His coming, Jesus will rescue us from the wrath that will follow (I Thess 1:10).
    (1) Christ speaks of the sudden appearance of a specific day in which we will be enabled to both stand before the Son of Man and escape all that is about to happen (Lk 21:34-36).
    (2) Christians will not experience God's wrath but His glory (I Thess 1:10; 5:9; II Thess 2:12-14).

    e. Paul relates our gathering to Christ with the Day of the Lord–speaking of them as though they were **A SINGLE EVENT** (II Thess 2:1-2; I Thess 4:16-5:2).

The Last Days

"The Rapture occurs before the Day of the Lord; in connection with the Day of the Lord; on the very day the Day of the Lord begins."

Rosenthal, "The Prewrath Rapture of the Church"

    f. Judgment will begin the very day the righteous are saved from the scene of impending destruction–"**Just as** in the days of Noah." "**Just as** in the days of Lot." (Lk 17:26-30).

    g. At a specific point in history ("day"), God will display His righteous judgment through both His kindness and His anger. He will reward those He has enabled to repent by His grace (the righteous), while displaying His indignation and fury against the wicked (Rom 2:3-11).

B. Intermission–God Inserts a Brief Recess Between Two Eras

The last days are even now being progressively unveiled as Christ breaks the first six seals on the scroll held in the right hand of the Father. The gathering of His Church will be the final act to follow the breaking of the sixth seal. Between the conclusion of this final event and the opening of the seventh seal (inaugurating the Day of the Lord), God will inject a brief intermission as described in **the 7th Chapter of Revelation.**

1. **Temporary Restraining Orders** (Rev 7:1-3)

    a. The four winds are prohibited from blowing–a worldwide calm is developed just prior to the storm.

    b. The angels empowered to injure the earth and sea (first 4 environmental judgments of the Day of the Lord) are ordered to delay their actions until God's servants are marked with the seal of God.

2. **The Saints on Earth are Introduced** (Rev 7:3-8)

    a. Their **number**: 144,000

    b. Their **nationality**: Israelites–12,000 from each tribe.

    c. Their **origin**: They most likely represent all, or a nucleus of, the survivors who escaped from Jerusalem at the end of the Great Tribulation.

    d. Their **status**: Already redeemed (Rev 14:3-4).

    e. Their **duty**: Servants of God.

    f. Their **protection**: Marked with God's seal (see Rev 9:4).

    g. Their **privilege**: To represent God in the Day of the Lord–a holy nation in the midst of a godless, condemned society.

    Note: All Jews living in the Day of the Lord are identified as belonging to God and related to Christ (Rev 12:17; 13:7; 14:3, 4; 15:2-4; 20:4).

3. **The Saints in Heaven are Introduced** (Rev 7:9-17).

    a. **Their number**: An innumerable great multitude.

    b. **Their nationality**: Representatives of every nation, tribe, people, and language.

    c. **Their origin**: Coming out of the Great Tribulation

    Note: All this host of believers will not necessarily enter into salvation during the tribulation period, or even be physically alive to experience or witness that trial, but they will all be raised to new life at approximately the same time that the tribulation terminates, and before the Day of God's Wrath begins.

    d. **Their identity: I believe this multitude represents THE ENTIRE CHURCH. Their united rapture will occur in such close proximity to that period known as the Great Tribulation that for all practical purposes they may be designated as those who have come out of that period.**

    e. **Their status**: Washed in the blood of Christ and robed with His righteousness.

    f. **Their garment**: Long white robes which exhibit the righteousness of Christ attained by cleansing with His blood. Evidently distinguishing them from even the angels who wear clean bright linen (Rev 15:6) (See also Rev 3:4-5; 19:7, 8, 14).

    g. **Their arrival in Heaven**: Rather recent. They were not present in the throne scenes depicted in Rev 4:2-7; 5:6-11.

    h. **Their favored position**: "standing before the throne and before the Lamb." It appears that this multitude may be in closer proximity to Christ than any of Heaven's other personalities who encircle the throne (Rev 4:4-6; 5:6, 11). The Church is close enough for Christ to "**spread His tent over them.**" This idiomatic expression can mean to take up residence or dwell with them. Another possible meaning is that He shelters them. In either case, it seems that they experience a favored and unique relationship with the Lamb. Before this multitude arrived in Heaven, we are informed that a sea of crystalline material occupied the area in front of the throne (Rev 4:6). The saints probably stand on this sea which reflects God's glory. Midway through the Day of the Lord, redeemed Jews will join them on this sea (Rev 15:2).

    i. **Their duty**: To serve God in His temple.

    j. **Their song**: "Salvation belongs to our God who sits on the throne and to the Lamb."

    k. **Their protection:**
       (1) In the Shadow of the Almighty
       (2) Sheltered from thirst, hunger, and discomforting rays (both ultra violet and infra red).

    l. **Their privilege** (for all eternity):
       (1) To be led by Christ
       (2) To share His blessings
       (3) To realize His comfort

4. The Two Congregations of Saints are Destined to be Separated for 3 ½ Years.

    a. **One left on earth to display His righteousness.**

    b. **One taken to Heaven to behold His righteousness.**

Period Two: The Day of the Lord

II. Period Two: The Day of the Lord

A. Introduction

The first phase of this period of wrath will immediately follow the rapture of the Church and be at least seven years in length. It will be ushered in by **THE OPENING OF THE SEVENTH SEAL** (Rev 8:1). The schedule, purposes, events, personalities, and places of paramount concern in that future period are revealed in **chapters 8-19 of the Book of Revelation**. The scenes previewed in that portion of scripture depict events transpiring in both heaven and earth, and for the most part are **revealed in chronological order**. These events follow those of the last days pictured in chapter 6, and precede the Millennium briefly referenced in chapter 20. The actual conclusion of the Day of the Lord will be postponed 1000 years until the completion of the earthly reign of Christ. At that time, God will finally terminate Satan's temporary sovereignty over the earth, crush sinful mankind forever (Rev 20:7-10), and even destroy the present universe because of its contamination by sin (II Peter 3:10-12). At the conclusion of the Day of the Lord, and perhaps considered by God to be a part of it, the Lord will sit on His throne to individually judge sinful mankind in its entirety, and sentence them to eternal death in the Lake of Fire (Rev 20:11). Then will follow a New Heaven and a New Earth where righteousness is at home (II Peter 3:13; Rev 21:1-22:5).

The following discussion of the Day of the Lord will focus only upon that major 7- year portion of the day, which begins immediately after the rapture and ends with the war of the Sovereign God's Great Day at Armageddon.

The sequential actions directed by the Lord during His Day are, for the most part, judgments upon an unregenerate and rebellious society and their satanic leadership. The peoples of all nations, except one, will be immersed in a sea of terror and excruciating pain as they are deprived of their environment, their possessions, their system, their cities, their health, and their very lives. Though a Satanic triad of evil seemingly experiences considerable success in dominating the earth and leading its citizens down the pathway of desolation, God never loses control, and in His time settles all accounts and brings about the destruction of these conspirators. **As irrevocable as God's grace is being distributed during the last days, so His wrath will be poured out in the Day of the Lord.** However, there will be a minority of participants in the Day of the Lord who will not experience its darkness, but be dealt with by the Lord in an entirely different manner. These are the Jewish survivors of the period of great tribulation; a remnant set apart and sealed by the Lord who will represent the only believers still resident on the earth during the Day of God's wrath. (Refer back to B2 on page 33).

These survivors will be entering the final seven years of a specified 490 year period of Jewish history in which God promises to accomplish a series of six objectives on behalf of the people and capital city of Israel (Dan 9:24). These objectives are (1) restrain transgression, (2) make an end of sins, (3) make reconciliation for iniquity, (4) bring in everlasting righteousness, (5) seal up vision and prophecy, and (6) anoint the Most Holy.

The first 483 years of this period was terminated by Christ's first advent (Dan 9:25, 26), at which time Messiah, through His death and resurrection, made provision for fulfilling God's first three objectives. Then began the last days, a transitional period of unspecified length, separating the first 69 weeks of years from the final seven years. As the last days conclude, the remnant will recognize and appropriate Messiah's provision for their sin, assuring their realization of God's first three objectives. Then they will make their entrance into the final scheduled week, assured that Christ will make His New Covenant prevail for them for the entire week. How He will accomplish this is discussed within the outline of Period II which follows. At the conclusion of the Day of the Lord, when Israel is established in righteousness in their promised inheritance, and the Anointed One sits on His throne in the Most Holy Place, God's final three objectives for His people will be realized.

B. THE FORECASTS OF THE DAY OF THE LORD

This period, also referenced in Scripture as the "Great Day of His Wrath" (Rev 6:17), and "the Time of Indignation" (Dan 11:36), is an important period of the end times which God actually planned from the beginning, as He has all His purposes (Is 46:10). Therefore, through His prophets, He faithfully foretold and warned of that future time when He would call men of all nations into account for their sins against Him. "The Day of the Lord" is a term used a total of 19x by eight different Old Testament prophets and 4x by three New Testament writers. None of these references attach any blessing to this period, other than its close proximity to Christ's return; contrasting the supreme relief of our final deliverance with the anguish of those left behind to face retribution (II Thess 1:6-10). **The Day of the Lord is exclusively spoken of as a time of devastating judgments** (Zeph 1:14-18).

1. **A Fearful Day** for mankind of every walk of life (Isa 2:12-21; 13:6-8). The Day of the Lord will arrive unexpectedly and the unregenerate will suddenly realized that they are in grave danger but have no options and no way of escape (I Thess 5:3; Zeph 1:18) The mourning the unregenerate will display at Christ's appearance (Matt 24:30) will quickly change to fear of such intensity that they will be driven to acts of desperation, both as they anticipate judgment (Rev 6:15-16) and as they actually experience it (Rev 9:6).

2. **A Day of Trouble and Distress** (Zeph 1:15)

3. **A Day of Travail** (Isa 13:6-8; I Thess 5:2-3)

    This will be the worlds' turn to experience severe birth pains; travail from which they will never gain relief and out of which spiritual life will never be conceived.

4. **A Day of War** (Zeph 1:16, Joel 2:1-11)

5. **A Day of Death** (Isa 13:9, 12; 34:2, 3; Zeph 1:17, 18)

    Note: If the descriptions of the Day of the Lord stopped at this point, we might be inclined to equate the consequences of the Day with the rides of the Four Horsemen during the period preceding

Christ's return for His own. However, there are further characteristics of that day which mark it as uniquely terrible:

6. **A Day of Spiritual Darkness "with no light"** (Amos 5:18-20; Zeph 1:15)

    a. Not darkness with a light in its midst (Phil 2:15)

    b. Not a day of darkness into which a beam of light may shine (II Cor 4:6)

    c. But darkness entirely void of light (Amos 5:20)

    d. Such a condition appears to be unique to the period of wrath into which earth's unregenerate inhabitants enter spiritually blinded and remain in darkness and gloom.

    e. The reason: All the lights are gone.
        (1) Christ, the Light of the world does not again manifest Himself to rebellious mankind until the very end of the seven year period (Rev 19:11)
        (2) The Holy Spirit has departed (II Thess 2:7)
        (3) The Church, through whom Christ reflected His Light (Matt 5:14-16), is in heaven (Rev 7:9-10).
        (4) The conscience within men's hearts has been snuffed out (Rev 9:20-21; Tit 1:15).

7. **A Day of Punishment for Sin** (Isa 13:11; 26:21; Obadiah 15; II Thess 1:8-10)

    This first seven-year phase of the Day of the Lord will not actually be the time of final judging and sentencing, but a time of **retribution.** God will confine to the Day of the Lord those He has already determined to be guilty, and upon whom He will administer the first installment of the punishment He has been patiently withholding.

    Note: The consequences of sin are even now being meted out as the Four Horsemen of the last days proceed on their circuit ride through the earth, utilizing mankind and nature to generate conflicts, catastrophes, and death. However these riders were not sent out to administer the final supernatural retribution, which will descend from heaven and ascend from the Abyss during the Day of the Lord.

8. **A Day of Vengeance** (God's) (Isa 34:8)

    After the rides of the Four Horsemen, martyred saints were still imploring the Lord to exercise vengeance on their behalf (Rev 6:10). In the Day of the Lord their prayer will be answered (Rev 16:4-7; 18:20, 24; II Thess 1:6, 7).

9. **A Day of the Lord's Anger** (wrath, indignation) (Isa 13:9, 13; 34:1-2; Zeph 1:15, 18; 2:2; 3:8)

    a. Probably no words describe that time better than "God's Wrath." During the Day of the Lord, He will unleash a wrath against sin which He has always had, (Rom 1:18) but out of concern for man's salvation, and because of His own great patience, has chosen not to fully vent (II Pet 3:9-10).

    b. All eight references to "wrath" in the Book of Revelation apply to the period which follows the opening of the seventh seal (Rev 6:16-17; 11:18; 14:10; 15:1, 7; 16:19).

    c. This is the wrath Christians will not experience (I Thess 5:9).

10. A Day of Destruction From the Almighty (Isa 13:6; Joel 1:15; Zeph 1:18; I Thess 5:2-3).

Unlike the period preceding Christ's return, when men will destroy each other through war and its consequences, during the Day of the Lord it will be God Himself directing the destruction.

11. A Day of Fire from the Lord (Joel 2:3)

From beginning (Rev 8:7) to end (Rev 20:9, 14, 15; II Pet 3:7, 12).

12. A Day of Desolation of the Earth (Isa 13:9; 24:1-3; Rev 11:18)

C. THE BEGINNING OF THE DAY OF THE LORD

1. **Preliminary Events in Heaven** (Rev 8:1-5)

    a. God's sovereign choice to begin this period of wrath will be declared in Heaven by **Christ's Opening of the Seventh Seal** (Rev 8:1).

    b. A half hour period of silence follows (Rev 8:1; Zeph 1:7)
       (1) Perhaps a reminder to heaven's host and ourselves of God's lengthy exercise of patience in restraining His wrath (II Pet 3:9).
       (2) A welcome opportunity for us to be still in our Lord's presence and appreciate Him all the more. In possession of pure and complete righteousness, the half-hour will contain more than 1000 earthly years of peace and joy.

    c. Preparations begin when the seven angels standing before God's throne are given seven trumpets (very likely by the Lord himself) (Rev 8:2).

    Note: Angels play a major role in initiating all the judgments of the Day of the Lord. By contrast, angels are not utilized to announce or initiate any of the catastrophes resulting from the opening of the first 6 seals, i.e.: occurring prior to the Day of the Lord.

    d. At the dawning of the day an offering is made to God:
       (1) An eighth angel with a golden censer is given a large quantity of incense to place upon the golden altar before God's throne, already laden with the prayers of the saints.

    Note: Prior to the rapture, martyred saints under this altar will petition God to exercise vengeance on resident's of earth responsible for murdering His people (Rev 6:10). These may be the prayers still on the altar, awaiting God's promised attention at the beginning of the Day of His wrath. Perhaps the vast quantity of incense supplied by God represents His own righteous demand for retribution. Subsequently, when He does administer such punishment to those guilty of murdering His saints, periodic approval from the vicinity of the altar will be heard—voiced by this angel, and perhaps saints in attendance as well (Rev 14:18; 16:7).

       (2) The smoke of the incense, mingled with the prayers of the saints, arises to God - magnifying and appealing to His righteousness.
       (3) The angel signals God's response, i.e.: His purpose to direct His wrath earthward, by filling the golden censer with burning coals from the altar and pouring them upon the earth.

2. **Arrival of Wrath to the Earth** (Rev 8:5)

    a. **Unexpected** to those who will be enveloped in it (I Thess 5:1-4; II Pet 3:10; Lk 21:34-36).

The Day of the Lord

   b. **Conspicuous** (II Thess 1:6-7)

   c. **Announced** by a special sign: A world-wide thunderstorm accompanied by an earthquake (Rev 8:5).

   Note: Periodically, and always at key points in the Day of the Lord, God will signify (confirm), through a special sign, that He is in control of the judgments directed at the earth. John first observed this special sign prior to the opening of the seals, when He beheld the throne of God in heaven. Proceeding from this throne came flashes of lightning, rumblings, and peals of thunder, all the ingredients of a gigantic thunderstorm (Rev 4:5). These phenomena were uniquely linked to the very throne of God Himself, clearly identified with His holiness, glory, and power. They represent a specific kind of signature which God will repeatedly attach to the manifestations of His righteous indignation at climatic points during the 7-year period of His wrath. These occur: (1) at the opening of the Seventh Seal, (2) at the sounding of the seventh trumpet (Rev 11:19), and (3) at the pouring out of the seventh vial (Rev 16:18).

God will underscore the progressive intensity of His judgments by including additional or enlarged phenomena each time He presses His signet ring into the wax of fresh judgments. When John first observed God's special sign, the thunderstorm was limited to visual lightning and audible thunder. When it is used to announce the beginning of the Day of the Lord it will include an earth quake. At the sounding of the seventh trumpet it will be intensified to include a gigantic hailstorm. At the pouring out of the seventh vial, both phenomena, the earthquake and the thunderstorm, will be intensified. The resulting earthquake is described as unprecedented in the history of the world, literally shaking down every island, every mountain, and every city. The accompanying thunderstorm will produce hailstones of about 100 pounds each, which will cause terrible damage and suffering as they come crashing down on mankind. Thus, God's signature will ultimately become a major judgment.

These repeated manifestations of God's glory and power, confirm the fact that the One who sits on the throne is the One in control of all the events of His Day. The similarities seen in the sign-judgments underscore the fact that the same Lord is executing all the various expressions of wrath that will be manifested in the Day of the Lord. The differences in the manifestations are consistent with the increasing magnitude of wrath He will display as His week runs its course.

In the final phase of the Day of the Lord, this dual sign will be observed for the 4th time when the Lord wipes out the rebellious armies of earth enlisted under Satan's control. In this final display of His wrath, the earthquake will be even more intense, and the torrents of rain and hail will be accompanied by burning sulfur, as well as other destructive forces (Eze 38:18-23). The fire from heaven will be the most severe of the forces unleashed by God, and will completely annihilate sinful mankind, i.e.: their bodies (Rev 20:9).

D. THE FIRST HALF OF THE DAY OF THE LORD (Rev 8:1-12:17)

1. **Sequential Judgments From God Are Inflicted Upon The Ungodly—Initiated By THE SOUNDING OF SEVEN TRUMPETS** (Rev 8:6-11:15).

   Note: during this first 3 1/2 years, judgments will be directed at those who lack God's seal (Rev 9:4). During the second half of the week of years, judgments will be directed at those who possess the mark of the Beast (Rev 16:2). The Chosen who bear God's seal on their foreheads will not be present in the latter period, and the ungodly will not yet bear the mark of the Beast in the former period. However, in both halves, God's wrath will be directed against the same crowd, those who are in rebellion against Himself.

a. **First Four Trumpets Sounded** - apparently in a relatively rapid sequence: **FOUR DEVASTATING JUDGMENTS—DIRECTED AGAINST THE ENVIRONMENT DESCEND FROM ABOVE** (Rev 8:6-12).
   (1) **First Trumpet**: The resident vegetation occupying 1/3 of the land mass of the earth will be burned up (Rev 8:7).
   (2) **Second Trumpet**: 1/3 of the sea devastated, including all resident creatures and occupant ships (Rev 8:8-9).
   (3) **Third Trumpet**: 1/3 of all streams poisoned (Rev 8:10-11).
   (4) **Fourth Trumpet**: All celestial lights dimmed by 1/3 of their intensity (Rev 8:12).

b. **Last Three Trumpets Sounded**—At moderately lengthy intervals: **THREE TERRIBLE WOES DIRECTED AGAINST MANKIND ASCEND FROM BELOW; FROM SATANIC ORIGIN** (Rev 8:13).
   (1) **First Woe** (5th Trumpet) (Rev 9:1-11).
      (a) **Origin**: The Abyss—unlocked by a fallen angel
      (b) **Agent**: Demons resembling greatly modified locusts.
      (c) **Appearance**: Powerful, attractive, terrifying.
      (d) **Leader**: Angel who governs Abyss, whose name is Destroyer.
      (e) **Mode of attack**: Stinging tails capable of injecting toxin that is excruciatingly painful.
      (f) **Length of time**: 5 months.
      (g) **Consequences**: Torture of such severity that men will prefer death.
   (2) **Second Woe** (6th Trumpet) (Rev 9:12-21).
      (a) **Origin**: A confinement and staging area near the Euphrates River.
      (b) **Agent**: A supernatural cavalry made up of two hundred million (200,000,000) horses and riders, organized into four divisions.
      (c) **Appearance**:
         - Riders in fire red, sapphire blue, and sulfur yellow breast plates.
         - Horses with heads resembling lions, mouths producing fire, smoke, and sulfur, and tails with biting serpent's heads.
      (d) **Leaders**: Four angels who had formerly been detained at that location; reserved by God for that very hour and purpose.
      (e) **Mode of Attack**: Murder of mankind by means of the lethal powers of the horse's mouths and tails.
      (f) **Casualties**: 1/3 of mankind will be killed

      Note: This figure is in addition to the possible thousands or millions killed within the previous few months by natural catastrophes (first 4 environmental judgments).

      (g) **Response of Survivors**: Unrepentant in respect to both their idolatry and their iniquity.
   (3) **Third Woe** (7th Trumpet) (Rev 11:15–18:24).

   Note: This final trumpet blast not only initiates the Third Woe for the unregenerate inhabitants of earth, but more importantly signals a complete changing of the guard relative to the administration of the earth. Satan, who has been allowed by God to rule over the unregenerate citizens of earth (Jn 14:30; II Cor 4:4; I Jn 5:19); to control his citizens and administer his Kingdom of Darkness from above (Eph 2:2); to continually access Heaven and to daily accuse those loyal to God (Job 1:6-7; Rev 12:10); loses his seat of authority in heaven and is cast down to the earth (Rev 12:9).

At the same time, Christ is given His rightful authority to assume dominion over the earth from Heaven (Rev 11:15-17). Christ's assumption of authority over the earth is directly linked with Satan's exile from heaven (Rev 12:10). Since Christ's reign will begin with the sounding of the 7th trumpet, it is assumed that Satan's exile from Heaven will also occur at that point. Though Christ's physical reign on earth will not begin for at least another 3 ½ years, the Lord will actually begin to call all the shots from the seventh trumpet on. During the period of the 3rd Woe, He will even use Satan to destroy the repulsive system of iniquity which the Devil himself has already established throughout the seven continents of earth; causing Satan to self destruct.

The portion of the outline, which immediately follows is limited to introducing **the negative consequences of Satan's demotion upon earth's rebellious society.** The positive consequences of Christ's exaltation, and in particular the activities of His chosen people and His messengers during the first 3 ½ year period, are identified in section 2 which follows the discussion of the third woe.

(a) The Third Woe is Personified by Satan
- The Devil and his host, composed of 1/3 of Heaven's angels (Rev 12:4), are defeated in a heavenly war with Michael and his angelic army (Rev 12:7-8).
- The losers are cast down to earth (eternally barred from heaven) (Rev 12:9).
- **"Be joyful you heavens"** (Rev 12: 10, 12 MLB). The scene will change from war in heaven to rejoicing in heaven. Even in heaven, the promised Kingdom in all its fullness of peace and joy had not been achieved prior to this point.
- **"Woe to the earth"** (Rev 12:12). Though Satan will have surrendered to Christ his official domination over the earth, his confinement to earth allows him to utilize and concentrate his remnant powers of deception and destruction at close range–a fact that assures that earth's inhabitants will suffer dire consequences as they become the victims of the Third Woe (Experience the results of Satan's presence and policies).

(b) The Third Woe is Initiated
- Satan realizes that his days are numbered (Rev 12:12).
- Therefore he immediately puts into action a plan to regain as much dominion and prestige as possible.
- His first priority is to eliminate Israel's remnant (Rev 12:13).
  - His initial attempts to exterminate them fail (Rev 12:14, 16).
  - Shortly before midweek he will regroup and invest his powers in a man through whom he determines to regain dominion over the earth and deify himself (Rev 13:1-4). Early in the second half of the week of years he will utilize this puppet to conquer the holy remnant (Discussed later on pgs 51-52).

(c) The Third Woe is Delayed
As noted above, Satan will first focus his attention upon Israel. Consequently, during the first half of the Day of the Lord, the ungodly citizens of earth will not experience or even anticipate the excruciating consequences of Satan's anxiety, anger, selfishness, and folly. It is during the final 3 ½ years that earth's inhabitants will experience the full impact of the Third Woe as they reap the terrible fruits of their allegiance to Satan and manipulation by Him (Rev 14:9-11; 16:2, 10, 11; 18:10, 15).

c. **During the First Half of the Day of the Lord, Additional Troubles will be Inflicted Upon the Ungodly by Two Special Messengers from God** (Rev 11:3-6, 11).
   (1) They prophesy to the people of earth for 3 ½ years–presenting a message the inhabitants refuse to accept (vs. 3).
   (2) Those citizens who openly oppose these messengers are consumed by fire, which issues from their mouths (vs. 5).
   (3) These Prophets have the power to scourge the earth through drought, transform any body of water into blood, and generate every kind of plague as often as they desire (vs. 6).

d. **The Reaction of the Surviving Ungodly to the Oppressive Judgments of the First 3½ years of Wrath.**
   (1) Express a desire to escape through death (Rev 9:6).
   (2) Exhibit no repentance from their perverted worship (Rev 9:20).
   (3) Exhibit no repentance from their polluted living (Rev 9:21).
   (4) Express enmity against God's messengers (Rev 11:9, 10).

   Note: Prior to the personal appearance of Satan, the unsaved express a steadfast resistance of God, but do not appear to openly attack Him. Perhaps it is because much of their early suffering is at the hands of satanic demons. However, beginning with the appearance of the Beast to slay God's messengers, their enmity against God becomes increasingly apparent, openly expressed during the vial judgments of the last 3½ years, and peaking at Armageddon.

2. **While Judgments Fall Upon the Unrighteous, Multiple Blessings from God are Bestowed Upon the Righteous.**

   a. **The REMNANT of ISRAEL:** An elect nation sojourn in a wilderness retreat for 3½ years.
      (1) **Their Origin:** The Survivors of the Great Tribulation
      (2) **Their Identity:** All true worshipers of God; an entire nation of believers in Christ who walk in obedience to their Lord (Rev 12:17). They are identified as "saints" (Rev 13:7; Dan 7:21, 25; 8:12) and "holy people" (Dan 8:24; 12:7). They are referred to as "blessed" (Dan 12:12). They are those who know their God (Dan 11:32). They have their reservations in for eternity (Dan 12:1). It is also possible that this remnant is referred to as "the Sanctuary" of God (Dan 8:11, 13, 14; See note regarding the human sanctuary on page 51).
      (3) **Their Covenant:** The Lord has promised to make His (new) covenant with this nation of survivors to prevail for an entire 7 year period, of which we are discussing the first half (Dan 9:27).
      (4) **Their Protection:** (Operation Desert Shield)
         (a) Shielded from God's Judgments (Rev 7:3; 9:4).
         (b) Separated from Satan's presence (Rev 12:6, 14).
         (c) Saved from Satan's power (Rev 12:15, 16).

   b. **The TWO WITNESSES of GOD:** Special ambassadors to Earth prophesy in Jerusalem for 3½ years (the first half of the Week).
      (1) Their message (Rev 11:3).
      (2) Their reception (Rev 11:5, 9, 10).
      (3) Their protective power (Rev 11:5, 6).
      (4) Their mission completed (Rev 11:7). (End of first 3½ years)

The Day of the Lord

      (5) Their apparent defeat (Rev 11:7-10) (Referenced on pg 51).

      (6) Their eternal victory (Rev 11:11, 12) (Referenced on pg 54).

    Note: These witnesses probably prophesy concerning the impending doom (clothed in sackcloth). Consequently the citizens of earth are vexed (vs. 10, see also Jer 25:30-33; 26:8, 9). As the world goes on trial, two key witnesses appear to level damaging charges. Rather than repenting and absolving themselves of guilt, earth's residents become implicated in murder when they celebrate the death of the two witnesses.

  c. **The CHURCH in HEAVEN** is provided a bonus of joy as they are forever separated from their accuser (Rev 12:10-12).

    Note: It appears that at the sounding of the seventh trumpet, the "good news" will attain a level of significance and fulfillment not previously realized.

  d. **The ANGELIC HOST of HEAVEN also rejoice**

      (1) Victorious in battle over Satan and his host (Rev 12:7, 8).

      (2) Their ranks purified as the polluters of heaven are cast out (Rev 12:9, 10, 12).

      (3) Celebrants at Christ's convocation to his rightful reign over the earth (Rev 11:15).

3. Sovereign Power is Exercised by the Lord during the First Half of His Day.

  a. He initiates all the transactions of that DAY when He opens the 7th seal (Rev 8:2).

  b. He controls the timing of judgments through trumpets He distributes to seven Angels (Rev 8:2).

  c. He controls the severity and determines the targets of judgments; even those delivered by demons (Rev 9:4, 5, 18).

  d. He controls all the behind the scenes preparations for judgments (Rev 9:15).

  e. He controls all the events of that Day, assuring that they harmonize with the Good News He gave His people through the prophets (His Word) (Rev 10:7).

  f. He controls the duration of all events (Rev 11:2, 3; 9:5).

  g. He delegates power to his servants (Rev 11:5-6).

  h. He overcomes His enemies, including death itself (Rev 11:10-12).

  i. He demotes Satan (Rev 12:9-10).

  j. He offers supernatural protection to His people (Rev 12:14-16, 6).

Note: Additional evidence of His control and power is demonstrated in the last half of His Day.

4. Glory and Honor are Given to Christ

  a. He is ascribed glory by those who oppose Him (Rev 11:13).

  b. He is thanked and praised by those who serve Him (Rev 11:16-18).

  c. He is exalted to His rightful position as Ruler over the earth (Rev 11:15; 12:10). The Father and Son assume sovereignty over the earth at the sounding of the Seventh Trumpet. Their authority will be immediately recognized and honored in heaven, though more than 3½ years will pass before Christ is enthroned upon the earth.

E. THE SECOND HALF OF THE DAY OF THE LORD–Including certain events that will occur around midweek

1. **A desolator takes the Spotlight on Earth's stage at Mid-Week**

   a. **His Name: Antichrist**–The prefix "anti" from a Greek preposition meaning both "against'" and "in place of." He will oppose and will exalt himself over everything that is called god or is worshiped, so that he seats himself in God's temple, proclaiming himself to be God (II Thess 2:4; see also Dan 11:36; Rev 13:5-8).

   He is also referenced as "the Beast," ("the Beast that comes up from the Abyss;" "a scarlet beast that was covered with blasphemous names and had seven heads and ten horns"); "the man of sin," "the adversary," "the lawless one;" "a hard-faced king," "the King of the north," "the Little Horn," "a desolator."

   b. **His Origin and Pedigree:**
   (1) **Arising out of the Sea of Gentile Nations** (Rev 13:1).
      (a) Bearing some of the characteristics and/or influences of several previous major world dynasties (all of whose domain had included Israel).
      (b) Bearing the greatest resemblance to the Greek Empire (Leopard).
   (2) **"Different:"** A direct characterization or reflection of the Roman Empire, which had the power to supplant all previous dynasties and to forcefully devour and enslave the entire civilized earth, imposing its own culture and standards upon the nations. This regime is identified in the Bible as "different" from former kingdoms (Dan 7:7, 19, 23).
   The Antichrist will gain at least a portion of his earthly dominion through conquest of several direct descendents of the Roman Empire (Dan 7:24). He will also display a brand of awesome power and authority resembling that of Rome, but actually surpassing it (Dan 7:20).

   Note: The 10 kings referenced in Dan 7:24 have their roots in 10 different segments of what had once constituted the Roman Empire. These individual provinces or nations are not necessarily European. In order to maintain control over its entire holdings, and facilitate effective and efficient government, the Roman Empire was divided into western and eastern halves in 293 A.D., and in 395 A.D. the two parts of the empire split apart. The eastern half actually persisted for 977 years longer than the western or European portion. At least some of the 10 kings who descend from the Roman Empire will probably be Middle Eastern leaders, and possibly all three of the rulers eventually subdued by Antichrist will, at the time of their defeat, be administrators of nations that originally were provinces or regions in the eastern half of the Empire.

   (3) **A "Different" Different–The Little Horn**
      (a) **The Little Horn of Daniel 7** (Introduced in Dan 7:8).
         Even though the Little Horn (Antichrist) will wield an authority representative of the powerful Roman Empire, he himself will not necessarily be genetically or politically linked to that regime. The Bible states that he will be **"different" from the 10**

The Day of the Lord

      preceding Kings of Roman lineage (Dan 7:24); probably in both character and roots (nationality).

  (b) The Little Horn of Daniel 8 (Introduced in Dan 8:9)
The Little Horn (Antichrist) is also identified with the Greek Empire; forecast to be a later day ruler of a partition of that kingdom recognized as the Seleucid Dynasty.

Note: The region controlled by this dynasty later became a part of the Roman Empire, and may eventually be taken back from three descendents of that Empire by the Little Horn.

The various individual rulers of the Seleucid Dynasty, during their respective reigns, were referred to in Scripture as "The King of the North" (See Dan chapter 11). These rulers, many of whom bore the name "Antiochus," were not descendents of Alexander the Great (Dan 11:4). Neither did they represent a continuous royal lineage, but included self made Kings of disreputable character (Dan 11:21). The worst of these Kings of the North was Antiochus Epiphanes, the Illustrious One, who was a forerunner and type of Antichrist.

The Beast (Antichrist) himself is referenced in Scripture as "the King of the North" (Dan 11:40). Thus, I believe he will have his roots in, and arise to prominence from, the region formerly identified as the Seleucid Dynasty.

Note: Though some things said about the Little Horn in Dan 8:23-25 were characteristic of Antiochus Epiphanes, he is not the primary villain depicted in this vision. It should be noted that this vision "relates to the final period" (vs. 17), and "the final events of the indignation time" (vs. 19) in the "distant future" (vs. 26). The final opponent of the Little Horn will be Christ himself (vs. 25). The period of history, the accomplishments, and the opponents, all relate primarily to Antichrist, as does also his final destruction by Christ Himself.

(4) A Different, Different, Different–A Unique Puppet of Satan.
The Antichrist will not only be a different kind of king ruling over a different kind of Kingdom, but he will be one of a select group of rulers whom Satan will set up and empower at various periods during the course of the world's history. The Antichrist, in addition to his Greek and Roman ancestry, will have Satanic roots.

In Rev 12:3, Satan is symbolized as an enormous red dragon with seven heads, each of them crowned, and ten uncrowned horns. We are not told in Scripture what these heads or horns represent. However, since Satan has been allowed by God to temporarily rule over the entire world, it is possible that his seven crowned heads represent his sovereignty over the seven continents of earth. We also recognize that from time to time, throughout world history, there have been rulers of demonic character whom Satan has controlled and used to promote his own evil program. Perhaps the seven crowned heads also represent seven super rulers, in the Devil's royal entourage, with whom he has shared his evil authority in unique ways.

The Beast, who is not pictured as a dragon but in many ways resembles the evil one who empowers him, is also identified as having seven heads and ten horns (Rev 13:1; 17:3). In Revelation 17:10-11, the seven heads of the Beast are identified as representing seven hills on which he resides, possibly symbolic of the seven continents of earth He will control (Rev 13:7b). They also represent seven unique rulers from whom Antichrist himself will spring as an eighth king. I believe it is possible that the uniqueness of this group of kings lies in the fact that they are all despots who have had, or will have, a common allegiance to Satan. Though their nationalities and periods of rule may be quite diverse, they are all demonically empowered by the Devil to demonstrate his ruthless character, claim deity, and blaspheme God (Rev 13:1, 5, 6). They likely share a common animosity toward the Jews, and are instruments used by Satan, through the ages, to persecute God's chosen nation. In the case of the Beast, the heads are not crowned for they do not represent rulers he controls, but rather a breed of perverted royalty from which he himself will arise.

At the time when the Apostle John received his revelation from Christ, five of the seven kings were already history (deposed of their thrones), one was reigning (Domitian?), and one was future. The latter is scheduled to arrive on the world scene for only a limited period of time (Rev 17:10). Terminating this parade of tyrants will come the Antichrist, an eighth King who is actually one of the seven. This relationship will be clarified in the next section.

His 10 crowned horns represent the 10 last minute, short term kings he will control (Rev 17:12-13). These puppet kings are described on pages 56 and 57.

(5) **A Different, Different, Different, Different**—Even among the seven Satan empowered tyrants, the Beast will be unique.

   (a) **He is the only one brought back to earth's surface from the depths of the Abyss** (Rev 11:7; 17:8).

   (b) **He is the only one who is mortally wounded and then brought back to life** (Rev 13:3, 14).
- Mortally wounded by the sword (vs. 14).
- Note that it is **one of the seven** heads of the Beast that is mortally wounded and then healed (vs. 3). Thus one of the seven prior rulers identified by these horns (Rev 17:10), one killed by a sword, will return to life as the Antichrist.

   (c) **He is the only wicked ruler who will be recycled, i.e., live and reign in two separate eras in history** (Rev 17:8, 11).
- The Beast is an eighth king but one who springs forth or belongs to the seven (He is the head among the seven that is mortally wounded and then healed). I interpret this relationship to mean that the Beast is actually a member of the original seven that Satan will utilize a second time to head up an eighth blasphemous regime.
- Since his original rule preceded John's lifetime ("once was"), he must be one of the first five tyrants who ruled at various periods during the eras preceding Christ's death and resurrection.
- Since he did not reign during John's lifetime ("now is not"), he is absent from earth during the foundational days of the church and in fact for the entire period of the last days–he is not a contemporary of ours, but will return to earth's surface and prominence from the Abyss.
- Since his reign will occur during the last 3½ years of human controlled government of earth (Rev 13:5), his second go-around ("and yet will come,") will occur in the Day of the Lord, after the sounding of the seventh trumpet and Satan's exile to earth.

   (d) **He is the only demonic ruler whom Satan invests with his complete power and authority**, even sharing his throne with the Beast (Rev 13:2). (Their resemblance exposed in Section d, pages 49 and 50).

The Day of the Lord

Note: It is likely that Antiochus Epiphanes is one of Satan's seven; tyrants who blaspheme God and persecute His people. Since Antichrist will have his roots in the Seleucid Dynasty, it is possible that the Beast will actually be the madman Epiphanes returning to earth's surface, the scene of his original crime. The only way a ruler from the seemingly extinct Seleucid Dynasty could overpower three decedents of the Roman Empire, which displaced it, would be to return from the dead. However, there is at least one fact about the Beast that seemingly does not fit Epiphanes. The Beast received his mortal wound by the sword (Rev 13:14). Historians tell us Antiochus Epiphanes died insane in Persia in 163 B.C., but the cause of death is not disclosed, perhaps because it was considered "natural." Because he had become an embarrassment to his regime, it is possible he could have been dispatched by an executioner's sword, but this is a mere conjecture.

c. **The Timing of His Arrival**:
  (1) He will be on hand at midweek:
    (a) To murder the Two Witnesses (Rev 11:7).
    (b) To begin his forty-two month administration of earth (Rev 13:5).
  (2) He may be on the scene earlier, in the first half of the Week.
    (a) It is possible there will be an interval of time between his ascent out of the Abyss (Rev 11:7; 17:8), and his rise out of the sea of nations (Rev 13:1).
    (b) Scripture indicates he may have a small (relatively inconspicuous) beginning and through time forcefully extend his geographical influence, eventually reaching greatness which extends even beyond the earth (Dan 8:9-10).
    (c) Such an introductory period would provide time for him to put down 3 Kings that are descendents from the previous Roman Empire (Dan 7:24).
    (d) His initial appearance could occur soon after the exit of the Holy Spirit at the beginning of the Day of the Lord (II Thess 2:7-9).
    (e) Could he have escaped the Abyss at the same time (5th trumpet) that it was opened to release a vast satanic force? (Rev 9:1-3).
    (f) The immoral and rebellious climate prevailing after the 2nd woe is completed, would seem to be a favorable time for his rise to power (Rev 9:20, 21). A climate of rebellion is definitely linked to his acceptance and success (Dan 8:12, 13, 23).

  Note: Though 1/3 of the vegetation, ocean life, fresh water sources, and human life will have been destroyed, both man and his environment in the balance of the earth may remain relatively intact, and ripe for satanic leadership.

d. **His (the Desolator's) Character**: Endued with the very nature of Satan.
  (1) **Possessing Satan's Throne** (authority)–the god of this world.
    (a) Delegated to the Beast (Rev 13:2, 4).
    (b) Recognized by the world (Rev 13:4, 8, 14).
    (c) Evidenced in his self-exaltation (Dan 11:36, 37). Expressing Satan's own ambition to exalt himself above the Most High (Is 14:12-14).
  (2) **Possessing Satan's Mouth** (Rev 13:5).
    (a) Designed to speak lies and deceive mankind
      - Just like his father (Jn 8:44).
      - Always opposing truth (Dan 8:12).

- **(b)** Depicted to have a mouth resembling that of a Lion, i.e. authoritative (Rev 13:2). The Babylonian Empire, unrivaled in the authority it exercised, was depicted as a lion (Dan 2:37, 38; 7:4, 17).
- **(c)** Dedicated to debasing God through blasphemy and slander (Rev 13:5-6; Dan 7:25; 11:36).
- **(d)** Directed toward self-exaltation–"boastful" (Dan 7:8, 11, 20).

(3) Possessing Satan's Power:
- **(a)** Unique:
    - Supernatural: invested by Satan (Rev 13:2; Dan 8:24; 11:39; II Thess 2:9).
    - Miraculous and Astonishing in nature (II Thess 2:9; Dan 8:24; Rev 13:13, 14).
    - Destructive, never constructive (Dan 8:24-25).
    - False and deceptive–"every kind of evil deception" (II Thess 2:9-11 NET).
- **(b)** Utilized (employed):
    - To gain prominence and deity (Rev 13:3, 13, 14).
    - To oppose God: His Christ, His people, His truth, His worship (Dan 8:12, 24, 25). Examples given in Sections e and f, which follow.
    - To defeat all opponents on earth (Dan 8:24).
    - To destroy even his own unsuspecting citizens (Dan 8:25; Rev 17:16).

(4) Possessing Satan's Skill:
- **(a)** A master of intrigue (Dan 8:23).
- **(b)** Successful in treachery (Dan 8:25).

(5) Possessing Satan's Temper (Wrath) (Rev 12:17; Dan 11:44).

e. **The Beast's Defiance of God**–In assuming the character of his master, the Beast shares the same enemies and hatreds. Clothed with Satan's power, he wastes no time in publicly displaying His enmity against God. "He opened His mouth to blaspheme God, and to slander His name and His dwelling place and those who live in heaven" (Rev 13:6). Then he takes up Satan's war against God's representatives on earth.

f. **The Beast's Early Conquests**–Perhaps the Beast's first demonstration of his destructive power is the murder of the two special envoys of God who will preach to the ungodly and unreceptive citizens of earth during the first 3 ½ years of the Day of the Lord. Then He will focus upon the Jewish remnant, the only entity remaining on earth that represents the true God and His Christ (Rev 13:7; Dan 7:21). The Beast is determined to remove the last remaining island of worship of God, and reverse the direction of all organized human worship to himself.

(1) The **CAMPAIGN of Antichrist** Against God's Agents and His People has been prophetically charted in Dan 8:9-12.
- **(a)** His rise to power includes the extension of his dominion toward the Glory Land (vs. 9).
- **(b)** To prevent heavenly intervention, he will destroy some of the angelic host and trample upon them (vs. 10). In the interpretation of the vision, given in Dan 8:15-26, this host is referred to as "**mighty opponents**" (vs. 24 MLB). It is possible these opponents are the 2 powerful witnesses he overcomes in Jerusalem. If not, perhaps a contingent of angels acting as Israel's bodyguard.
- **(c)** He will then attack the last bastillion of genuine worship of Christ remaining on earth, "the holy people".
    - **Abolishing the daily public sacrifice** (of praise) to Christ (vs. 11).

Note: the sacrifice abolished is identified as one belonging to the Prince, i.e. Christ. It is not sacrifice as prescribed by Moses.

- **Bringing down the (human) sanctuary** in which the sacrifice is offered (vs. 11). In the interpretation of the vision, no mention is made of a "sanctuary," but instead a synonym is used to identify the object of the Little Horn's destructive attack, "he shall destroy mighty opponents also the **holy people** (the remnant)." Israel will represent God's dwelling place on earth during the first half of the Day of the Lord, i.e. they will constitute Christ's earthly sanctuary. It is this people that Antichrist will temporarily humble, and thus succeed in cutting off their daily sacrifice of praise from the earth.
- **Eventually acquiring the daily sacrifice for himself** (vs. 12).

  Note: The entire sequence of events included in Antichrist's campaign against Christ's people and their worship of Him will occur "at the time of the end" (vs. 17), "in the time of wrath" (vs. 19 NET); the same period referenced as the time of Antichrist's self exaltation (Dan 11:36).

(2) The Beast's Conquests begin at Midweek
  (a) The ministry of the Two Witnesses will be abruptly terminated at the end of 3½ years (Rev 11:3, 7-10). Their period of ministry coincides with the first half of the week. It appears the Beast throws them down in order to set himself up (Dan 8:10, 11). Thus his attack upon this team of messengers will occur shortly prior to his recognition as the world's god. At the time of their murder, the assassin is identified by neither his rank nor his achievements, but rather by his origin: "The Beast that comes up from the Abyss…" (Rev 11:7).
  (b) The attack upon Israel, which is preceded by the restraint of the two messengers, is prophetically predicted to be initiated around midweek.
  - The Beast will be allowed to overcome and victimize the saints for 3½ years (Dan 7:25).
  - Christ will allow Israel's worship to be interrupted at the midpoint of their 70th Week, though He will continue to confirm His covenant with His people for the entire Week. This interruption coincides with the arrival of a desolator (Dan 9:27).
  - According to His plan, the Lord will relinquish the special earthly protection He will provide His people during the first half of the week (Dan 9:27; 7:25; Rev 12:6, 14).

(3) The Beast Accomplishes a Physical Victory Over the Saints Within a month and a half.
  (a) His victory is decisive–described in terms that depict the gravity of Israel's temporary defeat.
  - He will war against the saints and defeat them (Dan 7:21).

    Note: In vs. 22 Daniel continues: "…**until** the Ancient of Days came, and pronounced judgment in favor of the saints of the Most High, and the time came for the saints to possess the Kingdom." (subjects covered in Period III). Saints assuming such leadership roles in the Kingdom are identified as those who have been slain by the Beast and resurrected (Rev 20:4-6).

- The power of the holy people will be broken (**dashed in pieces**) (Dan 12:7).

    Note: It is interesting that Satan is able to empower a man to accomplish a task which he himself failed to do (Rev 12:15-17). Throughout history he has used human puppets to do his dirty work. Has God limited Satan's power so that he is obligated to channel it through human agents for certain tasks?

- He will "**overcome**" them (Rev 13:7 KJV).

    Note: the same Greek word, rendered "overcome", is used to describe: (a) the Beast's domination over the two witnesses whom he murdered (Rev 11:7); (b) the victory of the saints over Satan's accusations (Rev 12:11); and (c) Christ's ultimate victory over the Beast's armies (Rev 17:14). Thus this word carries the meaning of complete domination.

- "He shall **destroy**…the holy people" (Dan 8:24 MLB).

    Note: This same Hebrew verb is used to describe his treatment of "mighty opponents" (possibly the two witnesses), and later "the unsuspecting" (possibly Mystery Babylon whom the Beast will annihilate). The destruction of the holy people is limited to their physical state on the earth, from whence they go to heaven's glorious waiting room.

(b) The Defeat of the Holy People will probably occur **within 45 days of Midweek**. Dan 12:11-12 identifies two periods of time that follow the events that initiate the period of great misery to be experienced by the Jewish nation. The first **begins with** the abolishment of daily sacrifices and the setting up of the abomination that causes desolation. This period extends for 1,290 days, i.e. three years and seven months. If the tribulation period will last just 30 days beyond the events which trigger it, then the remaining 3½ years included in the 1,290 days would represent the first half of the 70th Week, and would terminate at midweek. The second period of 1,335 days runs concurrently and thus represents an extension of 45 days. If the end of 1,290 days does indeed mark midweek, then a month and a half later something that brings great joy awaits those reaching that date. I believe this promise is made to the remnant, and probably references the glorious reunion with Messiah that will be theirs (Rev 15:2-4). This blissful state will be attained following their physical defeat at the hands of the beast, thus his temporary victory over them would occur within 45 days of midweek.

(4) Completion of the Initial Campaign 110 days after midweek.
By the time he defeats the Holy People the Beast has accomplished most of his initial strategy. He has: (1) take the battle into the spiritual realm to defeat "mighty ones;" (2) suppressed the daily public worship of God from the earth; and (3) removed the last remnant of true worshipers. All that remains to complete the desolating reversal, which Antichrist desires, is to direct the world's worship to himself. This final objective will be accomplished in a relatively short time, so that within four months the complete strategy outlined in Dan 8:9-11 will have been successfully concluded. In Dan 8:13-14, a conversation between two angels is overheard in which the question of the duration of Antichrist's desolating program is raised and answered: Q: "How long shall the vision hold good?" (regarding all aspects of the apparent setbacks to true worship that will be experienced). A: "For 2,300 mornings and evenings, then the sanctuary will be re-consecrated" (Dan 8:13-14 MLB). I interpret

The Day of the Lord

this conversation to mean that the entire set of conquests accomplished by Antichrist will be valid for only 1,150 days before God reverses the tables, reestablishes His people on earth, and makes all things right in His Kingdom. Thus Antichrist will achieve his selfish ambition by effectively reversing worship 110 days after midweek. From that point until Armageddon, he will relish his temporary position as the world's god, and worship of the true God from the earth will be on hold.

Note: Two possible reasons why mornings and evenings are used to identify the duration of this period of time: (1) To provide an accounting of the times of true worship of God from the earth that will be temporarily eliminated, and (2) to account for similar times of worship directed to the Beast. When the Bible foretells the daily sacrifice being "taken away" from the Jews during their time of great misery, the word used to describe the action literally means "to turn off" or abolish. The word used to describe Antichrist's "taking away" of daily sacrifice is quite different, and actually means "to be high; i.e. to rise or raise." This action by Antichrist could be interpreted to mean that he will reinstate the daily sacrifices, diverting such worship to himself.

(5) **The Explanation of Defeat**—It Accomplishes God's will and thus is "**Allowed**" by Him.
  (a) In the accomplishing of His will, the Lord gives and the Lord takes away, and neither action diminishes His virtue (Job 1:21).
  (b) **The case of the Two Witnesses**:
  - "**I shall allow** My two witnesses to prophesy for 1260 days" (Rev 11:3 MLB). In the midst of their opponents they are given power that allows them to deliver their prophetic message without interruption, in its entirety, and within the scheduled time limit.
  - Then, on His schedule, God **allows** them to be overpowered by the Beast (Rev 11:7-10).
  (c) **The case of Israel**:
  - Kept in "a place prepared for her by God, where she might be taken care of for 1,260 days" (Noted in 2a on pg 44).
  - Then, on schedule (midweek), Christ will remove the fragrance of their sacrifice and offering from the earth (Dan 9:27). The "He" who will cause sacrifice and offering from His people on the earth to cease is none other than the "Messiah" of verses 25 and 26. He is not at midweek breaking His covenant with the Jewish elect, but will continue to confirm it ("make prevail") for the entire "seven," the latter half in heaven.
    - Dan 7:25 states: "**The saints will be handed over to him.**" Though it may appear that the beast is in control, the Lord, and not the adversary, will be moving the players to satisfy His own purposes.
    - Dan 8:12-13 reveals: "The hosts of the saints and the daily sacrifice will **be given over to it** (Little Horn)," and the sanctuary "**surrendered.**" The people of God (His sanctuary on earth), their daily worship of Him from the earth, and the angelic host who serve as their bodyguard, will all be temporarily surrendered to the Beast—but only temporarily!
    - Rev 13:7: "And he was **allowed** to make war against the saints and to conquer them" (MLB). Does it seem out of character for God to allow His people to be unjustly overpowered; to be humiliated by those who dishonor God; to be

cut off from daily communion with their Lord? If so, consider His treatment of His beloved Son. And, just as in the case of Christ, consider the final end of those who must suffer. ("Who, in view of the joy that lay ahead for Him, submitted to the cross, thought nothing of the shame, and is seated at the right hand of the throne of God." (Heb 12:2 MLB).

(d) The case of Messiah (Dan 9:25, 26 MLB).

- As predicted, "Messiah" arrives on earth's scene exactly sixty-two weeks (434 years) after Jerusalem is restored. He is honored, empowered, and protected by God until an appointed and prearranged time (Jn 7:30; 8:20; 12:23, 27; 13:1; 17:1).
- "but after the sixty-two weeks Messiah shall be slain, though there is nothing against Him".
  - "It was **the Lord's will** to bruise Him" (Isa 53:10 MLB).
  - "He was delivered up (to crucifixion) **in the determined will and foreknowledge of God**" (Acts 2:23 MLB).
  - "…against Thy holy Servant Jesus, **whom Thou dids't anoint**—Herod and Pontius Pilate with the Gentiles and the people of Israel, **all doing what Thy hand and Thy purpose preordained to take place**" (Acts 4:27, 28 MLB).

Note: God not only determined that Christ should be maltreated and murdered, but how it should be accomplished and by whom.

- "My God, My God, why have You forsaken Me?" The Father's temporary withdrawal, at the time of His Son's greatest suffering, was complete.

(6) The Consequences of Defeat By the Beast—"Death is Swallowed Up In Victory."

(a) The Two Witnesses will be taken to heaven in a cloud—in full view of their enemies who will be gathered together to celebrate their death (Rev 11:11-12). DEATH IS NOT DEFEAT IN GOD'S ECONOMY.

(b) The Remnant will also realize victory

- **Immediate Victory**: They are transported to heaven for the second half of their 70th Week. There the Lord continues to confirm His covenant with them.
  - Rendezvous with the Lamb on Mt. Zion (Rev 14:1).
  - Following the Lamb in Heaven (Rev 14:4). Their Shepherd as well as their Redeemer (Lamb).
  - All things made new:
    - A new song (Rev 14:3; 15:2-4).
    - A new location:
      - before the throne (Rev 14:3).
      - beside a crystal sea (Rev 15:2).
    - A new distinction: "first fruits (of Israel) to God and the Lamb" (Rev 14:4).
    - A new rest: "…that they may rest from their labor…"
    - A new annuity account: "…for their deeds will follow them" (Rev 14:13).
  - Acknowledged as Victors (Rev 15:2). **A physical battle was lost, a spiritual war was won.**

Note: It is unclear whether the 144,000 are taken directly to heaven without suffering death at the hands of the Beast or rather resurrected from death to make the trip.

Some who resist the Beast, and remain faithful to Christ, will surely face death prior to their subsequent resurrection and reward (Rev 14:13; 20:4). It is possible the martyrs referenced in these passages are additional members of the remnant who had sojourned in the wilderness, or more likely, that portion of the remnant who are carried into captivity during the great tribulation.
- **Subsequent Victory**: RESTORATION to their land and an earthly Kingdom (covered in period III).
  - The enemy defeated and destroyed (Dan 7: 26; 8:25).
  - The rights of the living sanctuary restored (Dan 8:14).
  - The Kingdom restored to its rightful citizenry (Dan 7:22, 27).
  - Antichrist's power over the holy people is exhausted at the end of his 3 ½ year reign (Dan 12:7).
- **Ultimate Victory**: POSSESSION of an eternal Kingdom (Dan 7:18, 32).

g. **The Beast's Apparent Success In Furthering His Agenda**–In addition to "prevailing against the saints," the Beast "shall do as he pleases" (Dan 11:36), and "shall succeed in whatever he undertakes" (Dan 8:12, 24 MLB).

(1) He deceives the whole world.
 (a) He throws truth to the ground (Dan 8:12).
 (b) "He causes deceit to prosper" (Dan 8:25). The Berkeley Version translates this phrase: "By his scheming he shall make the treachery that he applies win out." He even deceives himself into considering himself superior.
 (c) God allows him to delude unregenerate mankind. Since they would not accept the truth, God allows them to be vulnerable to falsehood. (II Thess 2:9-11).
 (d) He utilizes his right-hand man to further deceive earth's citizens (Rev 13:14).
 (e) He destroys the unsuspecting (Dan 8:25)–action identified in (6)(f) on page 61.

(2) He conquers the whole world.
 (a) He extends his authority over all humanity (Rev 13:7).
 (b) Conquering the mightiest of opponents (Dan 11:39).

(3) He controls the whole world.
 (a) Through the political system–by personal selection of the world's administrators (Dan 11:39).
 (b) Through the economy–by exercising absolute control over commerce (Rev 13:17).
 (c) Through military power
   - An extravagant military budget reflects his obsession with a quest for power (Dan 11:38).
   - He commands a lethal team of enforcers–(see h. (2), pages 56 and 57).

(4) He is worshiped by the whole world
 (a) He magnifies himself above every god, even the God of gods (Dan 11:36).
   - He ignores traditional objects of worship (Dan 11:37).
   - He opposes all so called gods (II Thess 2:4).

   Note: During the first half of the Day of the Lord, various forms of idolatry will flourish (Rev 9:20). However these will all be abolished by Antichrist.

   - He degrades the Living God (Rev 13:6).
   - "He seats himself in the temple of God with the claim that he himself is God" (II Thess 2:4 MLB).

- **(b)** He establishes a counterfeit religion.
  - He changes the timing and purpose of religious observances, and the content of religious guidelines (Dan 7:25).
  - He sets up a system of idol worship focused upon himself (Rev 13:14, 15).
- **(5)** His success will last until the indignation period is complete (Dan 11: 36).

h. The Beast Will Have Allies Who Strengthen His Position of Earthly Superiority.
- **(1) The False Prophet** (Rev 13:11-17).
  - **(a) Origin**: "out of the earth" (vs. 11).
  - **(b) Personality**: 2-faced. Appearance of godliness or meekness (lamb); but proclaiming a powerful satanic message (spoke like a dragon) (vs. 11).
  - **(c) Relationship**: A companion and spokesman of the Beast (vs.12). An integral member of the satanic triad (Rev 16:13).

    Note: Satan, during the period in which he will attempt to usurp the authority of the triune God, will operate on the earth as a triad of evil. By Satan's design, the roles and functions assumed by this triad will bear a certain similarity to those of the Holy Trinity. Christ carried out the Father's program (Jn 6:38, 40) through complete dependence upon His power (Jn 5:19, 30). Similarly, the Beast will be completely dependent upon Satan's power to carry out the Devil's program on the earth (Rev 13:2).

    Christ is to be honored on behalf of and to the same degree as His Father (Jn 5:23). Similarly, the Beast will share the worship afforded to Satan (Rev 13:4). A primary function of the Holy Spirit is to glorify Christ (Jn 16:13-14). A primary function of the False Prophet will be to exalt the Beast (Rev 13:12, 14).

  - **(d) Power**: Endued with the same satanic power as his superior, the Beast (vs. 12).
    - To perform impressive miracles.
    - To infuse the image of the Beast with vocal ability.

    Note: Satan was undoubtedly aware of God's pronouncement that idols were both deaf and **dumb**.

  - **(e) Mission**: To focus earth's attention and worship upon the Beast.
    - To act on behalf of the Beast.
    - To recruit worshipers of the Beast.
  - **(f) Methods**:
    - **Deception**: Through appearance (vs. 11), and miracles (vs. 13-14).
    - **Compulsion**:
      - Forced worship of the Beast (vs. 12).
      - Forced erection and worship of an image to honor the Beast–through threat of death for non-compliance (vs. 14, 15).
      - Forced reception of the mark of the Beast–through economic sanctions (vs. 16-17).
- **(2) Ten Puppet Kings**
  - **(a)** Foretold in the Old Testament (Dan 2:33, 41-44).

    Note: These 10 kings are those that make up **the iron portion** or the 10 toed feet that will be destroyed by Christ (Dan 2:34), but they are not synonymous with the 10 "former" kings of Roman Linage described in Dan 7:7, 20, 23-24. The Kingdoms of three of these former kings are actually annexed by the Beast, so that they, if still living, are his victims rather than his servants.

- **(b)** Represented in the symbolic description of the Beast in Rev 17:3, 7, 12.
- **(c)** They do not represent former kingdoms or any previous royal lineage–rather they are a surprise package of Johnny-come-latelys who will be anointed to share royal authority along with the Beast for the final 3 ½ years of the indignation period (Rev 17:12).
- **(d)** They are hand-picked by the Beast himself from among his most loyal devotees (Dan 11:39).
- **(e)** They are unconditionally and unitedly sold out to do the Beast's bidding and fulfill his ambitions (Rev 17:13, 17).
- **(f)** They are used to destroy Mystery Babylon (Rev 17:16).
- **(g)** They are assembled to lead the armies of the Beast against Christ (Rev 16:16; 17:14; 19:19).
- **(h)** They are put to death by the sword of the Lord (Rev 19:21)
- **(i)** Their flesh is then consumed by the scavengers (Rev 9:21).
- **(j)** They are ultimately relegated to the Lake of Fire (Rev 20:15).

i. The Beast Will Also Have Weak Allies Whom He Will Eventually Destroy.
  (1) Background
  - **(a)** Until his final judgment, Satan's objective will be to wrest mankind from God and to focus their attention and worship upon himself. (To "devour" them–I Pet 5:8; Eph 6:11, 12; Acts 8:23; Lk 22:31; I Jn 5:19).
  - **(b)** Prior to his exile to earth, Satan's principle strategy in achieving this goal seems to be to exploit man's inner sin nature, utilizing the attractions of the world to produce a citizenry that resembles himself, ie, a people who honor him by displaying his very nature: self-centered, deceitful, envious, covetous, greedy, full of iniquity, and anti-Christ (Jn 8:44; Eph 2:3; 4:17-19).
  - **(c)** To sustain and prolong such an orientation of society, Satan has currently arranged a union (marriage) of worldly influences, sensual appetites, and demons (James 3:15). The result is a powerful and mysterious infrastructure of wickedness; secular humanism mixed with idolatry and sorcery (Gal 5:19-21; II Thess 2:7; Phil 2:15).
  - **(d)** The product of Satan's labors through this established system of iniquity is presently, and will increasingly be, a materialistic and reprobate society dedicated to fulfilling the lust of the flesh, the lust of the eyes, and the pride of life; abandoned to shameful passions; sensual; wicked (Rom 1:21-32; I Jn 2:15, 16).
  - **(e)** During the first half of the Day of the Lord the earth's inhabitants will be characterized by their idolatry, self-gratification, violence, and unrepentence (Rev 9:20, 21).
  - **(f)** Thus, when the Beast is released from the Abyss, he will be welcomed by a society of rebels who have already been thoroughly indoctrinated in Satan's program of degradation. Iniquity and selfishness will actually reach a pinnacle of intensity at about the same time that the Beast is exalted to the position of worldwide dictator and god. In fact, international rebellion against God will help pave the way for Antichrist's acceptance as earth's potentate (Dan 8:23; Matt 24:12).
  (2) The powerful, yet veiled, infrastructure of secular humanism will still be in place in the Kingdom of the Beast, actively operating to promote, propagate, and satisfy the sensual desires of earth's inhabitants (Rev 17:4, 5).

- **(a)** This system is symbolized as "**the Great Harlot,**" and identified by the compound title "**Mystery, Babylon the Great, the Mother of Harlots and of the Abominations of the Earth.**"
- **(b)** The character of the Harlot is despicable:
    - **Immoral**–Promoting the lusts of the flesh (Rev 17:2, 4; 18:3). Supporting the merchandising of the bodies and souls of men (Rev 18:13).
    - **Abominable**–(Rev 17:4, 5). A favorite hangout for evil spirits and detestable things (Rev 18:2).
    - **Antagonistic and Murderous**–Promoting a spirit of anti-Christ (Rev 17:6).
    - **Self Centered**–Glorifying self (Rev 18:7).
    - **Self-Confidant**–Assured of superiority, fulfillment, and security–"I sit as queen, I am no widow, I will never see sorrow" (Rev 18:7 MLB).
- **(c)** But she is very **seductive** possessing a poisonous charm (Rev 18:23).
    - Attractive–dressed in wealthy attire and adorned with elegance and glitter (Rev 17:4; 18:16).
    - Alluring–holding forth a gold cup full of abominations and impurities (Rev 17:4), that the nations find irresistible (Rev 18:3).
- **(d)** She has **a long history of sinful accomplishments** prior to the last 3 ½ years.
    - Leading all the nations astray (Rev 18:23).
    - Murdering God's servants (Rev 18:24).

(3) The location of Babylon the Great in the Day of the Lord.
- **(a)** Will this system be centered in a **single metropolis**? Certain references to the harlot could be interpreted to infer that this evil force is indeed located in a single great city of commerce.
    - A specific city identified (Rev 17:18, 18:10, 16, 18, 19, 21).
    - Clues given to its general setting:
        - In a wilderness (17:3).
        - Occupying seven hills (17:9).
    - Symbolically referenced as a singular person:
        - "The Great Harlot" (Rev 17:1; 19:2).
        - "The Woman" (Rev 17:3-4).
        - "The Mother" (Rev 17:5).
        - Use of many singular pronouns in Rev 17, 18, 19.
- **(b)** Will this system rather be located in **multiple centers** of influence worldwide?
    - The harlot resides on many waters (territories) occupied by many nationalities (Rev 17:1, 15).
    - Her influence is international (Rev 17:2, 5; 18:23; 19:2).
    - She occupies seven hills–quite possibly a symbolic reference to the seven continents of earth (Rev 17:9).
    - She has historically exercised dominion over the rulers of the earth (Rev 17:18).

    Note: Dominion of the earth, or large portions of it, has historically shifted from one nation and capitol to another so that no single city could claim to have exercised such continual authority and influence.

    - When she is ultimately destroyed, there will be no alternative markets for the produce and wares of the earth's merchants (Rev 18:11-13). For such a void to be produced

The Day of the Lord

would require the destruction of all major centers of commerce, not just a single one.

Note: Merchants internationally are included in her citizenry–"Your merchants were the world's great men" (Rev 18:23).

- At her destruction, the smoke of her conflagration will be personally witnessed by leaders, merchants on land, and mariners at sea from many vantage points worldwide (Rev 18:9, 15, 17, 18). The references to all these men distancing themselves from the conflagration would be possible if they were viewing the destruction of a single city on screens located in many remote locations, but more likely this action indicates that all the witnesses were in the proximity of danger zones, and therefore took precautions to avoid frightening consequences in their own various backyards.
- No single location on earth can claim to have been the site of martyrdom of God's servants or to be their graveyard (Rev 18:24).
- Satan is accused of overthrowing the world's cities (Isa 14:17).
- The extension of Satanic influence is related to a worldwide web of cities (Isa 14:21).
- The Lord's judgments will be worldwide, extending to all the nations (Isa 14:26).

(c) The mysterious infrastructure of iniquity to be judged and destroyed by God will be international in scope (Rev 19:2) but it may very well be structured around a single prominent world center ("Great City"). This center, as well as a diversified network of metropolitan areas ("cities of the nations") will all collapse when God judges "Babylon the Great" (Rev 16:19).

- The singular person (great harlot) to be judged probably represents the entire wicked system (infrastructure) rather than a single center of commerce devoted to breeding and feeding sin.
- A future "Great City" could possibly occupy the former site of Babylon and Babel. It's mother status may reference the fact that, following the flood, the entire system of secular humanism seemed to begin with Babel, and spread out internationally from that city (Gen 11:1-9).
- There are other possibilities for "the Great City," including New York City, a current leader in world-wide commerce and secular pleasures, and the headquarters of the United Nations. The principle trade language of the World Wide Web is currently English. Of course the mystery concerning the identity of Babylon the Great will not be unveiled until a future time, but probably not very distant in the future.

4) **The Influences of Mystery Babylon Upon Earth's Inhabitants.**
   (a) Citizens of all nations will have been seduced by her to acts of passionate immorality (Rev 18:3).
   (b) All of earth's rulers (with the exception of the ten super kings) will have entered into illicit relationships with her (Rev 18:3), and be under her dominion (Rev 17:2, 18).
   (c) Earth's merchants will financially benefit from the abundance of wantonness she stimulates in society (Rev 18:3).
   (d) The love of Babylon the Great, by vast numbers of earth's inhabitants, is evidenced by their sorrowful reaction to her eventual destruction (Rev 18:9, 11, 18-19).
   (e) Their preoccupation with the affairs of Mystery Babylon is of such a magnitude as to seriously distract from their loyalty to the beast and worship of him. **Thus these subjects**

make up the weak clay in the feet representing the Kingdom of the Beast (Dan 2:41-43).

(5) **The Relationship between Babylon the Great and the Beast**
  (a) They share a similar origin–both being empowered and employed by Satan.
  (b) Historically Babylon the Great has been a working partner of seven preceding relatives who also served Satan. These included the Beast himself in his previous role on the earth (Rev 17:3, 9-11). [For clarity refer back to pages 47 and 48]
  (c) In the eyes of most of earth's inhabitants, the relationship between the Beast and Babylon will initially appear to be amiable and cooperative.
   • The Beast undergirds the harlot (Rev 17:3).
   • The harlot conducts her commercial transactions according to the Beast's rules (Rev 13:16-17). (He seemingly gets his recognition and she is able to satisfy her desires).
  (d) However, in the eyes of Satan and the Beast, Babylon will be a rival, because Satan will change both his program and his partners.
   • Knowing that his time is short (Rev 12:12), Satan's strategy will change. Through the Beast, he will seek to make himself, and not things or other idols, the supreme focus of mankind; to deify himself.
   • The preoccupation of men with achieving the sensual goals fashioned by Babylon seriously interferes with their whole-hearted commitment to the Beast, and obscures their perception of his claimed deity. Thus a system designed to seduce men from God, threatens to seduce them from Satan.
   • Consequently, this system is hated by the Beast and his cohorts, and he determines to destroy it (Rev 17:16).

(6) **The Judgment of Babylon the Great** (Rev 16:19).
  (a) **Her Judge is the Almighty Lord** (Rev 18:8).
   • He has all the facts needed for conviction–recognizes that "her sins are piled up to heaven" (Rev 18:5).
   • He determines her guilt (Rev 18:20).
   • He arranges for her destruction (Rev 17:16-17).
  (b) **A dual charge is made against her** (Rev 18:23-24; 19:2)
   • The corruption of earth's inhabitants.
   • The murder of God's servants.
     ▲ Evidences found that she is a serial killer (Rev 18:24)
  (c) **A just payment is required** (Rev 19:2).
   • Commensurate with her crimes of sensuality and self-glorification a double payment will be required (Rev 18:5-7).
   • Payment will also be required as retribution for the blood of God's servants (Rev 19:2).
     ▲ This judgment will not only reflect God's personal wrath (Rev 16:19) but will be meted out on behalf of His servants (Rev 18:20).
     ▲ By exacting this retribution, God fulfills His promise to martyred saints whose spirits cried out from beneath the altar of God (Rev 6:9-11).
  (d) **The payment is exacted in full**.
   • Her torture is excruciating (Rev 18:7-8, 10, 15).

- Her destruction is complete (Rev 17:16 MLB).
  - **"Makes desolate and naked"**–stripped permanently of all the wealth accumulated through a life of depravity (Rev 18:17).
  - **"Her flesh consumed"**–death of the inhabitants responsible for plotting and promoting her course of iniquity (Isa 14:22).
  - **"Burned up with fire"** (annihilation)–all remnants of her existence are erased, including the tools(means) for continuing or renewing her sinful occupations (Rev 18:8, 14, 21-23). "I will sweep her with the broom of destruction" (Isa 14:23).
  - Reverts to "the possession of wild animals" (Isa 14:23).
- (e) **The payment is executed swiftly**
  - A single **"day"** of torture (Rev 18:8).
  - A single **"hour"** of destruction (Rev 18:10, 17, 19).
- (f) **The executioner used by God murders his own people** (Rev 17:16; Isa 14:20).
  - The victims of the destructive judgment upon Babylon the Great were all citizens of the Beast's unregenerate kingdom, who had voluntarily accepted and borne his mark.
  - The Beast's displeasure with them stems from their allegiance to the very lusts which Satan had cultured and promoted within them.
  - They had no advance clues of his treacherous intentions (Dan 8:25).
  - This is the classic example of **Satan fighting against Satan**. Jesus stated that such action would result in self-destruction (Matt 12:25, 26). This is the beginning of the end for Satan and his puppets (Dan 11:44, 45).

(7) **The Reactions to Babylon's Destruction**
  (a) The world's reaction: **"Woe, woe, woe"**–recognition of the third woe.
   - great fear of experiencing similar torture and extinction (Rev 18:10, 15).
   - great sorrow over the loss of wealth and economic opportunity (Rev 18:9, 11, 19).
  (b) Heaven's reaction: joy and praise (Rev 19:1-5).

  Note: Quite a contrast to the earlier cries for justice which arose from under the altar (Rev 6:9-10). The former resentment will be replaced by rejoicing.

j. **Cracks Appear in the Superstructure of the Beast's Kingdom As It Approaches Collapse.**
  (1) Loss of population–accelerated premature deaths occur throughout the Day of the Lord, including those inflicted by the Beast Himself (Isa 13:12; Rev 9:18; Isa 14:18-20).
  (2) Loss of control–turning on his own citizens as described in the preceding section.
  (3) Loss of support–citizens of earth recognize that his actions are responsible for their personal deprivation (Rev 18:11, 15, 19).
  (4) Loss of environment–the policies and activities of the triad of evil bring about the destruction of the earth they sought to rule over–"…those who are destroying the earth" (Rev 11:18; Isa 14:16-17; 24:4-5, 19-20).

2. **The Earth Becomes Fully Ripe For Harvest.**

   a. Phase One of Harvest: **The Reaping of the Righteous** (Rev 14:14-16).
   (1) A promise is given in advance of eternal rest and reward (Rev 14:12-13).

Note: The recipients of this promise are likely the Jewish remnant, who though physically defeated by Antichrist, are spiritually victorious over him [As previously presented on pages 54 and 55—section (6)(b)].

- **(2)** The righteous will be personally harvested by Christ (Rev 14:14). Though he wields a sharp sickle His purposes are good!
- **(3)** The righteous are deposited before the throne of God on a sea of crystalline glass, to eternally sing His praises (Rev 15:2-4). The crystalline sea beneath their feet reflects the very glory of God, emanating from His throne (see Rev 4:3, 5, 6).

b. Phase Two of Harvest: **The Reaping of the Unrighteous** (Rev 14:17-20).
- **(1)** A pronouncement is given in advance of eternal unrest and torment for all who accept the Beast's claims upon their lives (Rev 14:9, 10).

  Note: The eternal condition of those who will make such concessions contrasts greatly with the eternal condition of those who are victorious over the beast (Rev 15:2). The former group will have no respite, day or night (Rev 14:10-11), while the latter are promised complete rest (Rev 14:13).

- **(2)** God will implement a very thorough and severe harvest of the wicked. [3x reference is made to the sharpness of the sickle used to symbolically picture the reaping of the wicked by an angel (Rev 14:17-18)].
- **(3)** The harvested grapes, representing the wicked, will then be thrown into the winepress of God's wrath and crushed. The resulting huge deposit of blood may depict the countless loss of life that will result when God expresses His wrath through His terminal judgments.
- **(4)** The harvest and crushing of the wicked will be accomplished during the final judgments of the Day of the Lord (described in the following two sections, 3 and 4).

3. The Final Demolition Begins–THE SEVEN BOWL JUDGEMENTS

a. The bowl judgments consummate God's wrath and are a seven-fold expression of it (Rev 15:1; 16:17).

Note: The War of the Sovereign God's Great Day, which follows the outpouring of this series of judgments, could be considered an additional expression of God's wrath (Rev 19:15). However, the stage is actually set for this war when the sixth bowl is poured out (Rev 16:12-14).

b. The entire sequence of bowl judgments originate and are executed from within the Heavenly Temple of God.
- **(1)** Seven angelic messengers, each bearing a specific plague, come out of the Temple, the heavenly Tent of Testimony (Rev 15:5, 6).
- **(2)** Then, one of the four living creatures delivers to these angels seven golden bowls filled with the righteous wrath of God (Rev 15:7). Evidently God's wrath is mixed undiluted with the plagues, ie. with the selected methods of punishment (see Rev 14:10). The impact of the plagues upon mankind is thus magnified, and God's justice is satisfied.
- **(3)** The release of God's wrath will express such a pronounced degree of His glory and power that the temple will be filled with smoke, and no one will be able to enter therein until the seven plagues are completed (Rev 15:8).

The Day of the Lord

Note: God's wrath, expresses and promotes His righteousness, and thus brings Him glory. It is the opposite of man's wrath, which fails to demonstrate righteousness and is demeaning to God and man (James 1:20).

(4) From within the temple, God's order is given to empty the bowls of God's wrath upon the earth (Rev 16:1).

c. The Seven Bowls are Consecutively Poured Out.
   (1) **The First Bowl is Emptied on the Earth** (Rev 16:2).
      (a) The Plague: loathsome and malignant ulcers.
      (b) The Victims: all who bear the mark of the Beast and worship his statue (see also Rev 14:9-10).
   (2) **The Second Bowl is Emptied on the Seas** (Rev 16:3).
      (a) The Plague: all salt water turned to blood.
      (b) The Victims: every creature of the seas.
      (c) The Result: annihilation of marine life.
   (3) **The Third Bowl is Emptied on the Rivers and Springs** (Rev 16:4).
      (a) The Plague: all fresh water sources are turned to blood.
      (b) The Victims: those who have shed the blood of saints and prophets.

   Note: Quite possibly all of earth's remaining unregenerate population share the guilt of such murder, at least indirectly.

      (c) The Result: they are forced to satisfy their thirst with blood (Rev 16;5-7).
      (d) The Response: the angel controlling these fresh waters considers such treatment a just recompense to these murderers. This concept of God's justice is also acknowledged with approval by voices in the vicinity of the altar. The latter approval is quite possibly expressed by those martyrs who previously entreated God to avenge their murder (Rev 6:9-10).
   (4) **The Fourth Bowl is Emptied on the Sun** (Rev 16:8-9).
      (a) The Plague: terrible, searing solar heat is focused on the earth.
      (b) The Victims: the general population of earth.
      (c) The Result: mankind is scorched.
      (d) The Response: the victims blaspheme God's character and refuse to glorify Him through repentance.
   (5) **The Fifth Bowl is Emptied on the Throne of the Beast** (Rev 16:10-11).
      (a) The Plague: the entire kingdom is plunged into darkness.
      (b) The Victims: all the citizens of his kingdom (probably earth's entire population at that future time).
      (c) The Result: Excruciating pain is experienced.

   Note: The darkness probably intensifies the pain already being suffered as a consequence of the previous plagues. It would make treatment of their wounds and alleviation of pain practically impossible, and further aggravate men's suffering by exposing them to serious injuries as they grope and flounder in the darkness.

      (d) The Response: Blasphemy of God's exalted position and continued un-repentance.
   (6) **The Sixth Bowl is Emptied on the Euphrates River** (Rev 16:12).
      (a) The Plague: The River is completely dried up.

(b) The Purpose: To facilitate the movement of Asian armies through the Middle East to a rendezvous with western armies in Israel, thus hastening God's plan for the subsequent destruction of these armies.

Note: The prior catastrophic changes that have occurred on earth have undoubtedly limited the means and routes of transportation quite drastically. Perhaps Satan musters earth's armies together in the spring of the year, when the Euphrates would ordinarily reach flood proportions and mountain passes further north would still be blocked by snow and ice. Under such conditions mass movement of ground troops from the far east to the Holy Land would be virtually impossible without the drying of the Euphrates.

(c) The Result: God's enemies accelerate their plans to combine earth's armies for an assault on Christ. They thus facilitate their folly and hasten their doom.

(d) The Response: evil spirits are dispersed by the Triad of Evil to muster the armies of earth's ten Super Kings to Armageddon, in preparation for the War of the Sovereign God's Great Day (Rev 16:13, 14, 16).

(7) The Seventh Bowl is Emptied into the Air (Rev 16:17-21). As the atmosphere encloses the earth, so the final bowl judgment will envelope the entire world, bringing the most inclusive, extensive and severe plagues of the entire series.

(a) The Announcement: lightning flashes, rumblings and thunder peals (see page 41—2c).

(b) The Plagues: a storm and earthquake, both of monstrous proportions and international in scope.
- The most severe earthquake ever historically experienced on the earth.
- The storm consummates in a fearful downpour of huge hundred pound hailstones.

(c) The Results:
- The earthquake levels all of earth's cities and splits the Great City into three parts, thus concluding the destruction of Babylon the Great.

    Note: "The Great City" is most likely Mystery Babylon, (Rev 17:18; 18:2, 10, 16, 18, 19, 21–refer back to discussion on pages 58-59 for the possible identity of this city). Jerusalem is also referred as "the great city" (Rev 11:8).

- The quake also drastically rearranges earth's landscape and seascape (The mountains crumble and fall, and islands disappear into the seas).
- The hailstones bring severe suffering and death to the survivors of the earthquake, who will have been deprived of normal shelter.

(d) The Response: Surviving humanity curses God for bringing the terrifying plague of hail. (Even though the earthquake will bring world-wide devastation, it appears that mankind will view the hailstorm as an even more fearful event).

Note: In the Biblical record of the final seven judgments, God is 3x recognized by the victims as the source and controller of these plagues. However, rather than glorifying Him through repentance, they curse Him each time (Rev 16:9, 11, 21). There is no question that mankind will recognize who is behind the judgments of the Day of the Lord (Isa 30:30).

The Day of the Lord

4. **The Final Demise of the Beast and His Kingdom–"THE WAR OF THE SOVEREIGN GOD'S GREAT DAY" (Rev 16:14, 16; Rev 19:11-21)**

    a. **Foretold:** Old Testament prophecies which foretell the successes of the Beast, also predict his destruction.
        (1) He will make great boasts, but be silenced by a just and speedy execution, ordered by "the Venerable One" (Dan 7:8-11).
        (2) He will enjoy dominion over the earth for 3.5 years, but then be consumed for all eternity (Dan 7:25, 26).
        (3) He will challenge even the Almighty, but be destroyed by Christ (Dan 8:24, 25).

        Note: The Scripture makes it clear that the Beast's downfall will come at the hands of Christ. Thus supernatural power will account for both His rise to power (energized by Satan), and his demise (destroyed by Christ).

    b. **Advance Recruitment of the Beast's Army**–see the preceding discussion of the 6th Bowl Judgment on pages 63-64.

    c. **The Composition of the Beast's Army**
        (1) It is international in scope, including the forces of all 10 kings who collectively govern the world under the Beast's leadership (Rev 17:12-14; 19:19).
        (2) A large contingent of troops from the orient is identified (Rev 16:12).
        (3) Also tied to this army as probable key combatants will be troops from Magog, Meshech, and Tubal (Ezek 39:1, 2, 6). These geographical titles are derived from the names of the sons of Japheth, who founded nations along the northern coastline of the Mediterranean Sea that originally bore their names. The portions of the areas once occupied by these ancient nations are currently a part of modern Turkey, and they probably extended further north as well. At one time these regions in Asia Minor were included in the Seleucid Dynasty, and even later were a part of the East Roman Empire.
        The leader of this central contingent of the Beast's army is an individual referred to as Gog (Ezek 39:1). This name may possibly be a synonym for Antichrist himself, whose beginnings have been related, in the 7th and 8th chapters of Daniel, to both the Roman Empire and the Seleucid Dynasty. The nations identified above may correspond to his geographic base of operations.

        Note: There are definite similarities between the account of the battle at Armageddon, and the conflict described in Ezek 39. According to the latter, Gog and his armies are drawn into the mountains of Israel by God himself. At that time the area is apparently unoccupied by either human victims or opponents. The mystery of who this invading force has come to fight is quickly solved when the Lord strikes down the entire host, and calls on the predators and scavengers to feast on their bodies. At this point it becomes evident that the international alliance has come to confront the Lord God Himself. Following the victory, God brings Jacob back to himself from captivity and has compassion on all Israel. Thus the sequel of events corresponds to actions which God will take both during and following the battle at Armageddon (Rev 19:11-21; 20:4-6).

        By contrast, Ezek 38 quite accurately describes a later invasion instigated by Satan upon the unsuspecting people of Israel, then occupying unfortified towns with a long history of peace and prosperity. As in the conflict occurring 1000 years earlier (at Armageddon), the Lord completely destroys the invaders, but the methodology for accomplishing such annihilation is quite different. Compare this Ezek 38 sequel with the conflict provoked by Satan in Rev 20:7-10. The discussion of this final war is reserved for Period IV of this outline.

d. The Site of the Battle
  (1) Though the battle that finalizes the Day of the Lord is not entitled "Armageddon" in Scripture, this geographical location is identified as the site of the conflict (Rev 16:14, 16).
  (2) There is general agreement among scholars that the site of this war lies within the boundaries of Israel, but there remains some question as to its exact location.
  (3) According to some scholars, "Armageddon" comes from the Greek "Harmagidon" which transliterates the Hebrew words for Mount (har) of Megiddo. That mountain is near the City of Megiddo and the Plain of Esdraelon. This location would be approximately 65 miles north of Jerusalem.
  (4) Megiddo literally means "rendezvous." When combined with har (mountains), the compound title would seem to define a **meeting on the mountains**. Because of the vast size of the host mustered to war by the Triad of Evil, these armies are probably not concentrated on a single peak but spread over an entire range of hills or mountains. The concentration of the Beast's army upon the mountains of Israel would seem to be confirmed in Ezek 39. The forces led by Gog are brought by God to **"the mountains of Israel"** upon which they are slain.

e. An Eye-witness Account of the Battle by the Apostle John (Rev 19:11-21 NEB).
  (1) The scene of glory above–**"THEN I SAW HEAVEN OPEN WIDE, AND…"**
    (a) A RIDER ON A WHITE HORSE COMES INTO VIEW
      - His Appearance:
        - "HIS EYES FLAMED LIKE FIRE"–He is the **Truth**; the pure and all knowing God.
        - "…ROBED IN A GARMENT DRENCHED IN BLOOD"—He is **the Savior**; wounded for mankind's sins.
        - "…AND ON HIS HEAD WERE MANY DIADEMS"–He is **Lord**; appointed to rule over all.
        - "FROM HIS MOUTH THERE WENT A SHARP SWORD"–He is **Judge**; Equipped to exercise just retribution.
      - His Names:
        - Describe **HIS UNIQUENESS**–His crown inscribed with **A NAME ONLY HE KNOWS** (bestowed by the Father, and evidently more descriptive and precious than we can even comprehend).
        - Describe **HIS CHARACTER**–Recognized by His subjects as **"FAITHFUL AND TRUE."**
        - Describe **HIS GLORY** (the complete expression of God)–Called by the name: **"THE WORD OF GOD."**
        - Describe **HIS EXHALTATION**–His clothing inscribed with the title: **"KING OF KINGS, AND LORD OF LORDS."**
      - His Mission:
        - To display God's wrath against sin (**"JUSTLY HE WILL JUDGE"**).
        - To bring retribution to the nations (**"JUSTLY HE WILL WAGE WAR"**).
        - To establish His sovereign rule over mankind.

The Day of the Lord

- **(b) FOLLOWING CHRIST, ALSO MOUNTED ON WHITE HORSES, COME HEAVEN'S ARMIES** clothed in shining fine linen (cleansed at the expense of their bloodied leader). These special forces are called "chosen and loyal" (Rev 17:14). They support their Lord but do not appear to be a factor in the victory; in fact, no reference is made to their bearing any weapons.

  Note: This cavalry is most likely the Bride of Christ, who seemingly wear the same resplendent linen garments in battle that they wore to the marriage banquet shortly prior to mounting their horses [Rev 19:7-8; noted on pg 70,c(2)].

- (2) The scene of expectancy in mid air–"AND I SAW…"
    - (a) **…AN ANGEL STANDING IN THE SUN.**
    - (b) **"WHO CRIED ALOUD TO THE BIRDS FLYING IN MID HEAVEN"**
      These scavengers soaring in earth's atmosphere are invited to congregate for a banquet upon the flesh of slain warriors of every rank and social status. The outcome of this battle has been predetermined with certainty!
- (3) The scene of defiance below: **"THEN I SAW THE BEAST AND THE KINGS OF THE EARTH AND THEIR ARMIES MUSTERED TO WAGE WAR AGAINST THE ONE MOUNTED ON THE HORSE AND AGAINST HIS ARMY."**

  Note: It is evident that this host did not gather to fight one another (see also Dan 8:25; Rev 17:12-14).

    - (a) There is no evidence that this international army had time to mount any offensive action, or even make a single defensive maneuver, prior to their destruction. In fact, they have just experienced the 7th Bowl judgment which must have crippled these armies to some degree (Rev 16:16, 17).
    - (b) The Beast and False Prophet are seized and quickly flung alive into the Lake of Fire.

      Note: These are the first individuals relegated to the Lake of Fire. Though prepared in advance, it may be ignited by God at this time (see Isa 30:33).

    - (c) Their armies are personally executed by Christ, utilizing the sharp sword issuing from His mouth.

      Note: Those who reject the words of His mouth, will received a just retribution from that same mouth. In fact, one way or another, His Word will judge all who reject Him (Jn 12:48).

f. **A Summary Statement Concerning "The War of the Sovereign God's Great Day," Commonly Referred to by the Name of its Site as the Battle of Armageddon.**

There are several common misconceptions of Armageddon that are from time to time expressed by the secular news media. Among these is the idea that Armageddon will be the stage upon which mankind will demonstrate their ultimate capacity for evil and violence. This war is visualized by some as a confrontation between men in which they go after one another with all the hatred and weaponry they can muster. According to this viewpoint, Armageddon itself is the event which brings about the final desolation of the earth. Therefore, this war constitutes a demonstration of men's madness and serves no real purpose. The Bible paints a different picture of this event, and one which furnishes us with a purpose.

To begin with, Armageddon is not a confrontation between men. No atom bombs will be dropped. Not a shot will be fired. It is a confrontation between the spiritual leaders of righteousness and unrighteousness, God and Satan. It is a war which pits the forces of good against those of evil; the former led by Christ, arriving from heaven, and the latter being an international army led by Antichrist, assembled in readiness on the earth. The world's armies defend a population who will have already completely embraced Satan's philosophy in respect to total rejection and hatred of God. The outcome of the battle will determine the future spiritual condition of the world, as well as its spiritual and political leader.

One of man's current concepts of Armageddon has some validity. This conflict will probably result in the greatest single blood bath of all time! The entire horde deployed over earth's Mideast battlefield by the Antichrist will be slain within a relatively short time. So extensive will be the carnage that scavengers and predators, both birds and beasts, will be gathered by God from throughout the earth to devour fleshy portions of the bodies, thus preventing disease from reaching epidemic proportions. The complete disposal of the bodies will require a seven month cleanup by an entire nation, and the largest cemetery and mass burial in the history of mankind.

Armageddon will be an epitome of evil, because the forces assembled there by the evil one will come with the intention of combating a righteous God. However, evil in all its ramifications will, at that time, already be fully mature and deeply entrenched upon the earth. The world will already be a cesspool of iniquity, and the Antichrist will have already committed the most degrading sin imaginable by proclaiming himself to be God. Sin, subversion, and violence will have already peaked out. Armageddon will not be the apex of evil, but a judgment against it; the event which will turn the course of world history from iniquity to righteousness.

Prior to Armageddon, much of earth's population will have already been blown away; earth's cities will lie in ruins; its forests will have been burned, its rivers and seas polluted. This war will not bring the world to the brink of destruction, as many believe, for it will already lie desolate as a consequence of the action of sinners (Rev 11:18), and the judgments of God (Rev 8, 9, 16). This war is destined to deliver the earth from a final collapse and set it on the road to recovery.

At Armageddon, the world will be delivered from rule by Antichrist and cleansed for rule by Christ. The course of the current world for the next 1000 years will be turned from war to peace, from desolation to restoration, from poverty to prosperity, from iniquity to righteousness, from error and lies to truth. This war will mark a pivotal point in world history, when "the kingdoms of this world become the Kingdom of our God and of His Christ."

5. THE AGENDA OF THE BLESSED DURING THE SECOND HALF OF THE DAY OF THE LORD

a. In the introduction to the Day of the Lord presented earlier in this outline (page 37), the entire seven year period was identified as both: (1) a time of climatic rebellion and judgment, and (2) **a special covenant week for a remnant of Israel**. Then in the portion of the outline covering the first half of the week, activities and developments relative to both the world's judgment and the Jewish remnant's Divine protection were presented. However, the content of the discussion thus far presented for the second half of the Week have headlined the activities of the Beast and focused on the demise of a Satan-controlled world without much reference to the elect of God.

Aside from the account of the spiritual victory and multiple blessings of the remnant, following their physical defeat by the Beast (Rev 14:1-5; 15:1-4), the Scripture is silent concerning the activities of the redeemed until chapter 19 of Revelation. At that point, we read an account of events in heaven that appear to occur on the very eve of Christ's triumphant return to earth to defeat His enemies and establish His Kingdom.

b. Heaven Erupts with a final premillennial Hallelujah Chorus (Rev 19:1-8).
  (1) The stage is set for this climatic chorus by **a series of prior heavenly acclamations** which progressively attribute honor and glory **to the Lamb, and to God (the Father) upon His throne.**
   (a) Praise given at the beginning of the Last Days; immediately after Christ receives the Scroll from the Father (Rev 5:6-14).
   - In song, the Four Living Creatures and the Twenty-four Elders proclaim the Lamb's worthiness to open the seals of the Scroll. The basis of such worthiness is acknowledged to be the shedding of His blood to purchase men of every nationality to God, as well as equipping them for eternal service in a royal priesthood.
   - "The Lamb that was slain" is then further extolled by the entire throng gathered before God's throne: "myriads of myriads, and thousands of thousands of angels" join the Living Beings and Elders in recognizing the Lamb's legitimate claim to "all power, wealth, wisdom, strength, honor, glory, and blessing."
   - The praise proclaimed on this occasion is then expanded to include both **God the Father and the Lamb** as the honored recipients, and every created being as the conferrers of such praise.

   Note: At a moment in history (very possibly already past), the Spirit of God enlightens and controls the spirits of every creature in heaven, on earth, and under the earth, focusing their attention upon their Lord and enlisting their praise. At that moment, acknowledgement of God's blessing, honor, and glory is pronounced by His enemies as well as His citizens; even by those humans whose bodies lie in graves, those angels confined to the Abyss, and Satan and his rebel angelic consort still resident in heaven.

   Thus the One who created all things (Col 1:16), sustains all things (Col 1:17), and through the cross made reconciliation to Himself possible for all manner of creatures (Col 1:20), appropriately receives praise from His entire creation. This is not the last or only occasion when such universal acknowledgement of His Lordship shall be given (Phil 2:9-11).

   (b) Praise given immediately prior to the Day of the Lord (Rev 7:9-12).
   - Recognizing the goodness of **the Father and the Lamb** for authoring and paying the price of salvation.
   - First voiced by a great multitude who constitute the newly arrived Church in heaven.
   - Affirmed by the angels who then expand the praise to recognize God's worthiness to eternally receive all praise, glory, wisdom, thanks, honor, power, and strength.

   (c) Praise given during the Day of the Lord, at the time of the sounding of the Seventh Trumpet (Rev 11:15-18).

- The reinstatement (reincorporation) of the earth into the eternal Kingdom of their Lord and God is recognized in heaven with a loud proclamation (no longer dulled by the minor key of Satan and his consort).
- God is both worshipped and thanked by the Twenty-four Elders for exercising His power to assume His rightful reign, thus inaugurating a day of retribution:
  - A time of judgment.
  - A time to recompense all those who honor His name.
  - A time to destroy (inflict eternal misery) on those responsible for the destruction of the earth.

(2) The climatic Hallelujah Chorus rings out in heaven as premillennial events are concluded on the Wedding Day of the Lamb (Rev 19:1-9).

Note: Praise of the Father and Son thus precede (introduce) the arrival of:

- The Last Days,
- The Day of the Lord,
- The assumption of Christ's sovereign rule over earth's Kingdoms, and
- The Millennial Kingdom

(a) The First Stanza of the final premillennial chorus looks back at God's conclusive judgment of Mystery Babylon (Rev 19:1-4).
- A vast throng shout a voluminous double "Alleluia" glorifying God for the power and justice He displayed in avenging the blood of his saints, and bringing eternal destruction upon Babylon.
- The conclusion expressed by the great multitude is then confirmed by the Twenty-four Elders and Four Living Creatures who add a spontaneous "Amen, Alleluia."

(b) The Second Stanza of the final premillennial chorus focuses not on His elimination of evil but His preparations for Eternal Righteousness (Rev 19:5-7).
- It is initiated by a solicitation from the throne for praise of God by all His servants.
- All of heaven's occupants respond to this invitation by praising God for two acts in particular:
  - The King has claimed His throne–"Alleluia"
  - The Lamb has claimed His bride–the chorus thus introduces the commencement of a joyous event in heaven.

c. The Wedding Celebration of the Lamb takes place (Rev 19:7-9).
  (1) In addition to being a special time for recognizing the glory of the Groom, it will be a time of exceeding great joy by the Bride.
  (2) Not only is the Groom recognized to be supremely worthy, but the Bride is observed to be ready–bedecked with the garment of righteousness provided by her Groom (see also Rev 7:9, 14; Isa 61:10; Phil 3:9).
  (3) Invited guests will attend the wedding feast, and every such guest is assured by God's Word of supreme happiness (Such joy as we would associate with that of the Bride herself.)

Note: There is some difference of opinion among Bible scholars as to the relationship between "the Bride" and "the invited guests." Some believe that these titles refer to two separate groups, while others believe the guests are individual Christians who collectively constitute the Bride (Church). I tend to agree with the latter opinion. However, it may very well be that the guests do represent a separate group of saints, namely the Jewish remnant. We know that the 144,000 will be with the Lord in heaven at that time (Rev 14:1, 3), and possibly additional Jewish victors over the Beast (Rev 15:2-4). It is unclear to me whether they will be present at the feast in glorified bodies, or whether their resurrection is still pending (Rev 20:4), but they never-the-less will be on hand to partake of the delicacies of the wedding feast. The timing of this event is such that all of the elect of God will be present in heaven as participants.

Note 2: The possible presence of two distinct groups at the wedding raises a question concerning the long-term, status of the elect redeemed. We know that up to a point, God has a different itinerary for the remnant Jewish nation that He does the Church. In this outline we have already noted such differences during the time of Great Tribulation, during the Day of the Lord, and at the beginning of Christ's earthly Kingdom. In fact, during the entire Millennial Kingdom, special promises, relationships, and activities will apply to the Jewish nation (addressed in Period III of the outline). Also, Satan's final attack will be directed at the nation and people of Israel (See Period IV). However, in the final analysis, when time has finally wound down, and all the redeemed are present in a **new heaven** and a **new earth**, I don't believe we will any longer be separate entities. God will bring all together in Christ (Eph 1:10). There will be differences among individual Saints, relative to rewards, but these distinctions will be based on prior faithfulness to Christ and not on race or former religious differences. The following statements of Biblical fact point out a few of the similarities between the Church and the Elect of Israel relative to their eternal status and relationship to God.

(a) Both are dependent on **faith in Christ alone** for their salvation (Rom 1:16; Jn 14:6; Jn 1:12; Acts 4:12; Zech 12:10; 13:1; Rev 12:17).
(b) Both will be created into **a single new person** (Eph 2:15).
(c) Both are reconciled to God **in one body** through the cross (Eph 2:16).
(d) Both have access to God **through one Holy Spirit** (Eph 2:18).
(e) Both will be **indwelt by God** in the person of the Holy Spirit (Eph 2:22; Acts 2:38-39).
(f) Both are participants in the **same New Covenant** (first given to the Jews–Heb 8:10-13; 10:16-17).
(g) Both will **personally know God** (Jer 24:7; 31:34; Jn 17:3; Heb 8:10-11; Eph 4:13; I Jn 5:20).
(h) Both are considered "**first fruits**" to God (James 1:18; Rev 14:4).
(i) Both are referred to as God's "**elect**" (Isa 45:4; 65:22; Col 3:12; I Pet 1:1, 2).
(j) Both are referred to as "**saints**" (Rom 1:7; Rev 13:7).
(k) Both are on God's schedule for a **similar salvation**, though different timing (Rom 11:25, 26).
(l) Both will be grafted as branches into the **same Vine** (Rom 11:17-24).
(m) Both will be **beneficiaries of God's mercy** (Rom 11:30-32).
(n) Both will ultimately be brought **together in Christ** (Eph 1:10).
(o) Both will enjoy **Christ's constant companionship** (Rev 7:15, 17; 14:4).
(p) Both, as citizens **together in Christ's Kingdom**, will be handed over to the Father's supreme authority by the Son (I Cor 15:24, 28).

- **(q) Both will occupy the New Jerusalem** whose foundation stones are represented by the names of the twelve Apostles, and whose twelve gates are designated by the names of the twelve Tribes of Israel (Rev 21:12, 14). It is interesting to note that the New Jerusalem will descend from Heaven as a bride adorned for her husband. Just prior to John's being taken to a high mountain, where he could view the descent of the New Jerusalem, he was told by His angelic guide that he was to be shown the Bride, the Lamb's wife (Rev 21:2, 9-10). The most unique thing about the New Jerusalem is not its dimensions, nor the streets of gold, but the fact that **the City's occupants represent the Bride of Christ**. To be sure, this Bride is represented by the Church, standing on the foundation of the Apostles and ultimately Christ Himself (Eph 2:20), but she is also represented by the twelve Tribes of Israel (Jewish remnant), who have entered the gates into the Bride's Chamber. Though formerly different, when God makes all things new the two groups become indistinguishable members of a single Bride, who is singularly loved by her Husband. God is not a polygamist.

d. **The Saints mount up, and follow the King of Kings on His return to earth to defeat His enemies and establish His Kingdom** (Rev 19:14). Identified earlier in (b) on page 67.

6. **POST WAR EVENTS**: Scenes of transition which closely follow the conclusion of the War of the Sovereign God's Great Day and set the stage for Christ's millennial reign on earth.

   a. **Satan's Imprisonment**: the Dragon is seized, bound, thrown into the Abyss, and securely incarcerated there for 1000 years. This temporary detention constitutes interim action taken to assure that he will be unable to deceive anyone on earth during this period of confinement (Rev 20:1-3). His final sentencing to eternal punishment will thus be postponed, but not in the least absolved or diminished (See Period IV). This defeat and internment of Satan will be commemorated in song (Isa 14:3-20).

   b. **God Sets Up a Sign Among the Nations** (Isa 66:19). This sign is possibly the resurrection of martyred Jews in the very midst of their former international oppressors–clarified in B.1.a of Period III–pg. 83.

   c. **Witnesses Carry the Message of Christ's Victory to the Nations** (Isa 66:19) By His grace, God spares a small fragment of the Beast's armies, and sends these survivors back to their respective lands to proclaim His glory (Through their first hand account of His glorious display of power and justice).

   d. **Christ Inaugurates His Government on the Earth**–seating those given His authority to judge (Rev 20:4).
      (1) Among those given positions of leadership are martyrs from the Day of the Lord (Rev 20:4, 5).
      (2) The Apostles of the Lord were promised special responsibilities as judges over Israel (Lk 22:28-30).
      (3) Others may very well receive similar assignments relative to the Gentile nations included in Christ's domain.
      (4) In fact, it is likely that all of the elect of God will not only serve Him, but share with Him in the administration of His Kingdom (II Tim 2:12; Rev 5:9-10; Dan 7:27).

e. **The Regathering and Regeneration of Israel**–Since this nation has already been chosen as the chief beneficiary of the Millennial Kingdom, and will play a key role in the administration of that Kingdom, one of the first priorities on Christ's agenda will be the return of this people to their homeland, as well as their spiritual renewal (Ezek 39: 25-29). This subject is outlined in Part B of Period III.

f. **The Initiation of Restoration**–The Cleansing of the Land begins with the disposition of the remains of the fallen army.
  (1) Widespread contamination is seemingly averted by utilizing thousands of predators and scavengers to consume the flesh of the slain prior to direct human contact (Ezek 39:17-21; Rev 19:17-18). This feast goes on for at least a year, both winter and summer (Isa 18:6).
  (2) The task of locating, removing, and burying the skeletons of the dead host is assigned to the restored nation of Israel.
    (a) For seven months all the citizens of the Land will be involved in burying Gog and his entire army in a valley east of the Dead Sea, formerly named "the Valley of the Travelers," but by God's design, renamed "the Valley of Gog's Horde" (Ezek 39:12-16). So immense will be this cemetery that major east-west traffic through this region will be impeded (Ezek 39:11).
    (b) After the seven initial months, a special task force will search the entire land for additional bodies, marking them for gravediggers who will then bury the bodies, thus completing the cleansing of the Land (Ezek 39:14-15).
  (3) Periodically the citizens of the nations are assembled in the Valley of Gog's Horde to view the grim results of God's justice, and to loathe those who rebelled against Him. They will also come to understand how God's glory is displayed through His just punishment of sin (Isa 66:23, 24; Ezek 39:21).
  (4) The weapons of the fallen army will be utilized as the primary source of Israel's energy for the first seven years of the Millennium (Ezek 39:9-10). Thus disposing of the junk while providing time for revegetation of the land, and the development of permanent energy sources from the abundance of natural resources which will characterize the rejuvenated land of Israel.

g. **Supernatural Changes in the landscape, climate, and resources of Israel** are accomplished by the Lord; assuring a level of productivity and prosperity never realized since Eden (Identified in Part C of Period III on pages 97 and 98).

h. **The balance of post Armageddon activities are presented in the concluding sections of the outline**. From the beginning of the Millennium to its end, Christ will be central and His glory, including all His attributes, will be revealed and demonstrated throughout the earth (Isa 11:9; Hab 2:14). A small sample of what this means to His chosen ones, and to a different degree the balance of earth's citizens, will be the subject of the outline presented for Period III.

Period Three:
The Millennial Kingdom

III. Period Three: The Millennial Kingdom

Marching Down The Last Corridor of Time

We will not comprehend the regal beauty of the King nor the scope and magnificence of His earthly Kingdom until we actually experience it. To adequately describe its beauty, justice, peace, and prosperity, and chronicle its progress through 1,000 years, would require the devoted and tenacious labor of hundreds of authors, poets, reporters, historians, photographers, artists, secretaries, and publishers; and their combined data, descriptions, and illustrations would probably fill thousands of volumes of books.

In the Biblical preview of the Millennial Kingdom, God has not seen fit to provide us with such voluminous manuscripts, but He has given us brief glimpses into that lengthy, spectacular, and eventful era of time. In the following outline, I will summarize a portion of this revelation under topics addressing various aspects of that period of Christ's earthly rule.

As you proceed through the condensed outline of Period III, keep in mind that this climatic 1000-year period is but a brief phase of God's eternal Kingdom. God has planned incomparably greater and more wonderful things for the post-millennial phase of His Kingdom, which will continue throughout the vastness of the infinity beyond time. "Behold, I will make all things new…these words are trustworthy and true" (Rev 21:5).

In the Millennial phase of the Kingdom, as glorious as it will be under Christ's administration, a portion of mankind will still experience imperfections, temptations, failures, punishment, defeat, and tears. Though these blemishes will not infect His saints, neither will they be completely removed from the earth by God, until the New Heavens and New Earth come into existence. Presently, many Christians look forward to the anticipated glory of the Millennial Kingdom, and so we should, but when we have experienced the greater glory to follow we will not even reflect on this past, or recall the events of those 1,000 years (Isa 65:17). In fact, the fondest expectations of current day believers will actually begin to be fulfilled prior to Christ's earthly reign (Rev 7:9-17), and continue to gush forth in overflowing proportions throughout the eternity that we spend with Him in the New Jerusalem; and wherever else our Shepherd may choose to lead us.

In its conclusion, the Book of Revelation focuses our attention upon the glory that lies beyond time, providing us with only a momentary glimpse of the preceding 1,000-year period. To be sure, it does call our attention to the blessedness of those who will participate in the first resurrection, and thus share in the government and priesthood of Christ during His earthly reign. However, this commentary is capsuled into just three verses, wedged between the accounts of Satan's imprisonment in the Abyss during the Millennial

Kingdom and his release at its conclusion (Rev 20:1-10). Until Satan, the instigator of sin, is finally cast into the Lake of Fire, the blemishes resulting from the blight of sin will still exist upon the physical earth and in the hearts of unregenerate mankind.

The spiritual and physical blessings of God's people, both Jew and Gentile, will indeed be glorious during the Millennial Kingdom, and the blessings resulting from Christ's righteous reign will also be realized to a lesser degree by the entire world (Psa 72:17). However, the state of the majority of earth's citizens, as well as that of their environment, will be far from perfect. That is not to say that Christ's government is imperfect, or that the Millennial Kingdom is not an important part of God's agenda. He has some specific purposes for that period which relate to both His own people, Israel, and the nations; some important lessons to teach mankind about Himself that have not previously been fully comprehended, as well as some misconceptions to erase. A feeble attempt to portray some of the objectives of God's orientation program during the Millennium is included in the following outline in section B.4, Fruition in the Land.

A. THE FOCAL POINT OF THE KINGDOM WILL BE THE KING

1. His glory will be acclaimed at His coronation in heaven

At the sounding of the seventh trumpet, when the Kingdoms of the world officially become that of the Lord (Father) and His Christ (The personage of the Trinity designated to exercise authority on the earth), the entire heavenly host (Satan and his angels having just been cast out) will praise God for assuming His great power and authority and beginning His reign (Rev 11:15-17; 12:10).

2. His glory will be manifested in His reign on the earth

   a. It will be the splendor of a King (Isa 33:17).

   b. It will be the glory of God Himself (Psa 50:2).

   c. It will be evident and acknowledged throughout the earth (Isa 11:9; Isa 52:10; Psa 97:1, 6).

   d. It will be of such magnitude as to humble His physical creation (Isa 24:23).

   e. It will be so radiantly glorious as to shame His enemies (Psa 132:18).

   f. It will be so awe-inspiring as to cause all nations to reverence His name (Psa 48:10; 99:1-3).

3. His glory will be consistent with His exalted position:

   a. "Exalted **in the earth**…" (Psa 46:10).

   b. "Exalted **among the nations**…" (Psa 46:10).

   c. Exalted (Supreme) **above all the nations** (Psa 72:9-11; 99:1-3; 47:2, 7).

   d. **The Lord will be sovereign over every office and aspect of international government**; His royal authority encompassing all three divisions of what many nations commonly conceive of as the major branches of government; i.e. administrative, legislative, and judicial branches (Isa 33:22).

   (1) **KING**: God will establish His own Son as King of Kings in Zion (**Psa 2:5-10**; 72:8-11; 97:1; Isa 33:17; Zech 14:9).

   (2) **LAWGIVER:** The Word of the Lord will become the Law of the Land. It will be taught by Christ in His Temple, and broadcast throughout the earth (Isa 2:2-3).

The Millennial Kingdom

Note: His covenant people will be unique in that they will have His law placed in their inner being (Jer 31:33).

(3) JUDGE: The Lord will be Chief Justice over all nations (Psa 9:4, 7, 8; 96:13). Psalm 9:7 MLB states, "**He has established His throne for judging.**" It is possible that the most demanding function of the King will be His role as international judge. Just and righteous decisions on behalf of individuals and nations will characterize and glorify His throne (Psa 96:10, 13).

4. **His glory (Holy attributes) will be evident as He conducts the business of the Kingdom (exercises His royal authority)** (Psa 48:1, 10).

    a. **Prepared to do business**: Uniquely complemented by the Spirit of the Lord who shall rest upon Him, providing knowledge, wisdom, understanding, counsel, power, and reverence of His Father (Isa 11:2).

    b. **His chief business**: "His delight shall be in the reverence of the Lord" (Isa 11:3 MLB).

    c. **Doing holy business**: Among the godly attributes conspicuously demonstrated in His reign will be (1) Righteousness, (2) Faithfulness, (3) Loving-kindness, (4) Peace, (5) Power, (6) Wisdom, (7) Grace, and (8) Joy. During the Millennium, the fruits of the Spirit will finally become the policy of international government.

    (1) **RIGHTEOUSNESS** will characterize Christ's reign
        (a) He is **the Righteous Branch** of David's royal line who God has promised to raise up (Jer 33:15).
        (b) He is endowed with **the righteousness of God** (Psa 72:1, 2).
        (c) He zealously pursues and promotes righteousness
            • The King's energy is "**keenly set on righteousness**" (Psa 99:4 MLB).
            • The King will "**seek righteousness and be eager to do it**" (Isa 16:5–Berkley). "…speed the cause of righteousness" (Isa 16:5-NIV).
            • "**In His days the righteous will flourish**" (Psa 72:7).
        (d) He demonstrates righteousness in His demeanor and actions:
            • An inseparable part of His being–"**Righteousness will be as a belt around his waist**" (Isa 11:5 NET).
            • The hand by which He will mold His kingdom–"**Your right hand is filled with righteousness**" (Psa 48:10).
        (e) He demonstrates righteousness in His decisions and judgments (Psa 9:8).
            • Righteousness and judgment are the foundation of His throne (Psa 89:14).
            • His judgments will provide sure help to the needy, afflicted and oppressed, as well as deliver swift punishment to evildoers (thus displaying both faces of the coin of righteousness) (Isa 11:4; Psa 72:4, 12-14).
            • His decisions will be based on Truth and not hearsay; what God wants, and not what people think (Isa 11:3, 4; Psa 96:13).
            • "**When your judgments come upon the earth the people of the world learn righteousness**" (Isa 26:9).
        (f) When He comes, He will shower mankind with righteousness (Hosea 10:12; Isa 45:8; 61:11; Psa 72:6, 7).
            • Righteousness will reside in His people Israel (Isa 60:21), who will address Him by the name: "the Lord our righteousness" (Jer 23:6; 33:16).

- Righteousness will be very evident in Jerusalem, His place of residence, which will be known as "the City of Righteousness" (Isa 1:26).
- Righteousness will be attested to by the productivity and beauty of the physical and biological creation (particularly within the land of Israel) (Psa 72:3).
- Righteousness will be appropriated to some degree by people of all nationalities (Isa 26:9).

Note: One of God's six primary objectives in His design for Israel is to "bring in everlasting righteousness" (Dan 9:24).

(g) The prevalence of righteousness on earth and its fruit of peace, will be the chief characteristics distinguishing the Millennial Kingdom from all previous eras of human history. However, the high level of righteousness achieved during that period will be surpassed considerably in the New Heavens and New Earth, where righteousness will really settle down and be at home (II Pet 3:13).

Note: In some of the preceding references, the Hebrew word for righteousness may be translated "justice."

(2) **FAITHFULNESS** will sustain all His decisions and actions. He will always keep His Word and act in accordance with it (Psa 119:138; 145:13).
   (a) Christ's exaltation **to His throne** will demonstrate the faithfulness of the Father (Isa 49:7; Jer 33:14).
   (b) Christ's rule **on His throne** will demonstrate His faithfulness (Isa 16:5).

Note: Faithfulness will so characterize the King that, figuratively:
- Faithfulness will be perceived to be a throneside servant (Psa 89:14) and,
- His royal wardrobe will be perceived to include a sash of faithfulness (Isa 11:5).

(3) **POWER** will be exercised by the King (Isa 40:10).
   (a) Power to initiate His Kingdom by raising citizens and administrators from the dead (Rev 20:4; Ezek 37:12-14).
   (b) Power to create beauty from chaos (in both humanity and their environment) (Isa 35:1-7).
   (c) Power to subdue His enemies (Psa 2:9-12; 110:2; Isa 11:4).
   (d) Power to protect His people (Isa 27:3).
   (e) Power to stabilize the world (Psa 96:10).
   (f) Power to produce prosperity (Psa 72:6-7, 16; Jer 33:9)
   (g) Power to produce a majestic Kingdom (Psa 145:11-12).
   (h) Power that evokes praise (Psa 68:32-35).

(4) **PEACE** will prevail during Christ's reign (particularly in Israel).
   REASONS FOR PEACE
   (a) **The presence of the King**–The Prince of Peace (Isa 9:6).
   (b) **The prevalence of RIGHTEOUSNESS**–peace will occur as a direct consequence of righteousness (Isa 32:17). Because righteousness will characterize the King and His people during that era, an abundant harvest of peace will be reaped in Israel, and exported to the entire world.
   (c) **The obstacles to peace will be removed by God**
   - Demonic power removed: Satan chained in the Abyss (Rev 20:1-3).

The Millennial Kingdom

- Destruction and violence are quenched by universal submission to the Lord's sovereignty (Isa 11:9- Net Bible).
- Dissolution of fear through installation of a caring and protective government (Jer 23:4; Micah 4:3, 4).
- Disturbance of the peace is minimized by removal of agitators (Isa 16:4, 5; Psa 37:9-11).
- Disarmament and demilitarization is completed as military hardware is converted to implements of productivity (Isa 2:4; Micah 4:3).
- Division between Israel and Judah is mended (Isa 11:13).
- Disappearance of predation by carnivorous mammals and attacks by poisonous reptiles–not by their destruction but by changing their nature and physiology (Isa 11:6-8).

(d) Arbitration of Disputes by the King results in the achievement of peace between nations (Isa 2:4).

ASPECTS OF PEACE:

(a) Peace with God–"I will make a covenant of peace with them; it will be an eternal covenant with them" (Ezek 37:26 NET).

Note: This covenant will be commiserated with the redeemed of Israel. However there will be those of other nationalities who will turn to God and become recipients of such peace (Isa 2:3, Zech 8:20-22).

(b) Peace with man
- Residential peace: peaceful homes (Isa 32:18) and peaceful backyards (Micah 4:4).
- Urban peace (Isa 33:20).
- National peace (Isa 11:13).
- International peace (Isa 2:4).

(c) Peace with nature
- The landscape becomes a "peacescape" (Isa 55:12-13).
- The wild animals become pets (Isa 11:6-9). The declaration of peace is extended even to the Animal Kingdom.

DEGREE OF PEACE:

(a) Enough to really relax (Micah 4:4; Isa 32:20).

(b) "Abundant peace" revealed (Jer 33:6; Psa 37:11).

(c) "Great peace" enjoyed (Isa 54:13).

ENDURANCE OF PEACE:

(a) Peace will persist despite adversity (Isa 32:18, 19).

(b) Peace will not be interrupted by Satan for an entire millennium (Rev 20:2, 3; Ezek 38:11).

(c) "Peace will prevail as long as the moon remains in the sky" (Psa 72:7 NET).

Note: We know that following the 1,000 years Satan breaks the peace and attacks Jerusalem, resulting in a catastrophic judgment from God that destroys his armies. As the earth is shaken as never before, and torrential rains, hailstorms, fire and brimstone descend from the heavens (Ezek 38:19-22), it is likely that the moon itself is literally removed. Its light and regulatory powers will no longer be needed for the time will have arrived for the current earth and its solar system to be dissolved, and be replaced with the New Heavens and the New Earth (Rev 20:11; 21:1, 23).

(5) The **WISDOM** of God will guide all the affairs of the Kingdom
   (a) The King will have the Spirit of Wisdom and Understanding (Isa 11:2).
   (b) He will rule with wisdom and understanding (Jer 23:5).
(6) **JOY** will be a common emotion expressed during Christ's reign.
   (a) **The Lord Himself** will rejoice in His people and in their habitation; both recreated for the purpose of being a delight to God (Isa 62:3-5; 65:18-19).
   (b) Those coming out of darkness will rejoice because the light of His presence makes them "very happy" and gives them "great joy" (Isa 9:2, 3 NET).
   (c) His special people, **Israel**, will rejoice from the first day they set foot back in Jerusalem (Isa 35:10; 51:11).

   Note: The scope of their joy will be identified later in Part B: The Honored Citizens of the Kingdom.

   (d) **Worldwide**: Joy in Christ's reign will spread to distant lands (Psa 97:1).
      • All nations will recognize the marvelous salvation and righteousness the King has wrought and brought to earth, and be invited to join in a symphony of Joy (Psa 98:1-9; 67:4).
      • Jerusalem and its Chief Occupant will be a source of joy for the entire earth (Psa 48:1-2).
   (e) **Earthwide**: Joy will infect all the physical and biological creation when the various parts are freed from the curse of sin to realize the fulfillment of their separate but harmonious functions (Rom 8:19-21).
      • Rejoicing in recognition that God has arrived in their midst to reign, and thus provided stability to earth (Psa 96:11-13; 98:7-8).
      • Rejoicing in recognition of their enrichment as a consequence of His presence and blessing (Psa 65:8-13; Isa 55:12).
      • Rejoicing in recognition that the Lord has shared with them a portion of His glory (Isa 35:1-2).
(7) **LOVING-KINDNESS, MERCY** and **GRACE** will not be forgotten commodities in the Kingdom. These virtues collectively characterize the benevolent manner in which the King will relate to His subjects.
   (a) His "throne will be established (set up) in **loving-kindness**", ie. from the beginning of His rule, loving-kindness will be manifested in the manner in which the King achieves His objective of righteousness (Isa 16:5 MLB).
   (b) The Millennial Kingdom begins when God extends His **mercy** (compassion) to Israel by bringing them home (Ezek 39:25-27).
   (c) "…the Lord longs to be **gracious** to you (Israel), He rises (from His throne) to show you compassion…How **gracious** He will be when you cry for help! As soon as He hears He will answer you" (Isa 30:18, 19).
   (d) Gentiles from various cities and nations will also come to Jerusalem to seek the Lord and receive His favor (Zech 8:20-22).
(8) **HOLY** is the term which will be used to identify the unique worthiness of Christ the King (Psa 99:3, 5, 9). The attributes of Christ presented in the preceding sections represent some

The Millennial Kingdom

of the components of His unlimited and eternal wealth of glory. This infinite and spotless glory is unique to God Himself, and thus **His position is separate and distinct from His entire creation. "HOLY" is the term used to identify this unique position of separation.** Holiness is not a single attribute of God, but rather a title identifying the total character of the One who possesses and exercises all the attributes that constitute true glory, without exception, reservation or termination. During the Millennium, all the nations will recognize His holiness.

(a) Holiness will so characterize the King, that the term "holy" will also be applicable to His place of habitation, His immediate surroundings, His personal possessions, His people, and His works. For example, in His Kingdom he will be described as sitting on a **Holy** throne (Psa 47:8), in a **Holy** temple (Psa 5:7), on the **Holy** Hill of Zion (Psa 2:6; 48:1), within the **Holy** City of Jerusalem (Isa 52:1), in a **Holy** section of the Land (Ezek 45:1).

(b) "The Holy One of Israel"–This title, used in reference to God, occurs numerous times in Scripture, and will finally be ascribed to Him by the entire international community. All the nations will so honor Him when they recognize the **distinct** glory He displays, and that is reflected through His **separated** people Israel (Isa 60:9, 1-3).

B. THE HONORED CITIZENS OF THE KINGDOM: ISRAEL

1. **Return to the Promised Land from Exile**
   a. **Resurrected**–prior to their regathering the Israelites must be resurrected (Ezek 37:4-14).

   Note: Living Jews probably will be nonexistent upon the earth during the final climatic events of the Day of the Lord. As already pointed out in preceding sections of this outline, the escapees of the Great Tribulation will eventually be conquered by the Beast (Rev 13:7), and probably killed (Dan 8:24). Those Jews carried into exile during the closing days of that same tribulation period (Zech 14:2; Lk 21:24), will probably also be killed for their refusal to comply with the Beast's demands. The only glimpses we snatch of Jews during the final half of the Day of the Lord, is of those who are either killed for their faithfulness (Rev 14:13) or redeemed from the earth following spiritual victory over the Beast (Rev 14:5; 15:2). The only Jews specifically identified for a special role in the Millennial Kingdom are a group who have been beheaded for choosing Jesus over the Beast. These are subsequently resurrected at the beginning of the Millennium (Rev 20:4). It is obvious that Jewish believers who lived in earlier eras of history have also died, and if chosen by God to be included in the regathering, must first be resurrected (Isa 26:1-3, the result of v19).

   (1) Their physical resurrection (vs. 8) will be accompanied by spiritual regeneration (vs. 14).
   (2) This resurrection will occur world-wide in the various lands where they have been scattered, and very possibly slain (vs. 9) and buried (vs. 12).
   (3) This resurrection will include multitudes of Jews (vs. 10). Their identification as "The whole house of Israel" probably refers to the fact that every tribe will be represented in this remnant (vs. 11).
   (4) This resurrection will occur preparatory to their resettlement in the land of Israel (vs. 12-14).
   (5) Daniel was told that he would rise at the end of time to his allotted inheritance (Dan 12:13).

- **(6)** Undoubtedly many O.T. believers will be included (Heb 11:12-16). These are those who, during their lifetime demonstrated faith in their God by exercising hope in a promised future inheritance.
- **(7)** Prominently included with the "old timers" in this resurrection will be Jewish saints who will have recently been martyred by the Beast (Rev 20:4).

    Note: Their resurrection is specifically identified as "**the first resurrection.**" This title is probably applicable to the resurrection of all true believers, i.e. the resurrection to eternal life (Jn 5:29; 11:25, 26; Dan 12:2). If so, then the resurrection of this remnant of Israel constitutes a second phase of "the first resurrection," the Church having already participated in an earlier phase (I Thess 4:16-17). Guaranteed benefits of the first resurrection include: happiness, holiness, freedom from the power of the second death, and the privilege and honor of serving God in His eternal Kingdom (Rev 20:6). These guarantees belong to every Christian as well as the Jewish remnant.

b. Regathered
- **(1)** The nations put on notice (Jer 31:10).
- **(2)** His people sought out by God (Ezek 34:11-13).
    - **(a)** Because of His special love for them (Isa 43:4-6), and their special status (Isa 43:7).
    - **(b)** In all places of their worldwide dispersement and exile (Ezek 37:21; Isa 27:12).
    - **(c)** For the purpose of returning them to their land and their Lord (Jer 32:37-39).
- **(3)** Called by a clear signal sent out to the nations into which His people have been dispersed (Isa 11:12).
    - **(a)** Perceived and responded to by His exiled people (Isa 27:13).
    - **(b)** Perceived and responded to by the peoples of the nations (Isa 49:22).
- **(4)** Demonstrating a rescue from the dominion of strong oppressors (Jer 31:11; Isa 49:24-26; Ezek 34:27b).
- **(5)** Delivered once and for all (Isa 45:17).

c. Transported back to their land.
- **(1)** From world-wide points of origin (Isa 43:5-6; 49:12).
- **(2)** "A great throng will return" including those with physical disabilities and limitations, and even some unborn (Jer 31:8). None of the elect are left behind (Ezek 39:28; Isa 43:7).
- **(3)** Overland routes are prepared to facilitate travel to Israel (Jer 31:21; Isa 49:11; 62:10). Ships will also be used for overseas transport (Isa 60:9).
- **(4)** They begin their journey with contrite and seeking hearts (Jer 31:9).
- **(5)** Enroute, they are guided, strengthened and refreshed by the Lord, who thereby exhibits His compassion and mercy (Jer 31:9; Isa 49:9-13).
- **(6)** They will be escorted and assisted by citizens of those nations who previously had been their captors (Isa 14:2; 60:4).
    - **(a)** Given preferential treatment (Isa 49:22-23).
    - **(b)** Provided with VIP transportation (Isa 66:20).

    Note: Former enemies, and not angels, are God's agents for aiding the return of His people. By way of contrast, at the rapture Christ will utilize a host of angels to bring the Church to Himself (Matt 24:31).

The Millennial Kingdom

2. **Arrival at Their Destination**

   a. **Reception**: "Open the gates, that the righteous people who maintain truth may enter in" (Isa 26:2 MLB).

   b. **Recognition**: "Look, here is our God!" (Isa 25:9 NET). Israel will meet the Lord in Jerusalem, and not in the atmosphere; on a throne instead of a cloud (Micah 4:6-7).

   c. **Response**:
   (1) Awe–"We thought we were dreaming" (Psa 126:1 NET).
   (2) Joy–"At that time we laughed loudly and shouted for joy" (Psa 126:2 NET).
   "…and they shall come and sing out their joy on the height of Zion, and beam for joy over the bounty of the Lord" (Jer 31:12 MLB) (See also Isa 35:10; Isa 51:11).

   Note: The contrast between the tears of contrition shed enroute to Jerusalem (Jer 31:9), and the joy of completeness demonstrated upon arrival, is very striking.

   (3) Commitment–"they will come and bind themselves to the Lord in a lasting agreement that will never be forgotten" (Jer 50:5 NET).

   d. **Report**: "At that time the nations said, 'the Lord has accomplished great things for these people" (Psa 126:2 NET).

   e. **Reflection**: "The Lord did indeed accomplish great things for us" (Psa 126:3 NET).

   f. **Request**: "O' Lord, restore our well being, just as the streams in the arid south are replenished" (Psa 126:4 NET). The Lord's response will have already been initiated.

3. **PLANTED IN THE LAND BY GOD**–Amos 9:15; Jer 33:14

   a. **The Lord affirms the planting**: "I will see to it that they (Israel) are built up and firmly planted. I the Lord affirm it" (Jer 31:27-28 NET). He promises to put His whole heart and soul into this project, and thoroughly enjoy doing it (Jer 32:41).

   b. **The Lord foretells the success of the planting**: "In days to come, Jacob shall take root; Israel shall bud and blossom and shall cover the face of the earth with produce" (Isa 27:6 MLB).

   c. **PURPOSE of the planting**: "They will be called Godly oaks, trees **planted by the Lord to reveal His splendor** (glory)" (Isa 61:3 NET).
   (1) God will reveal His splendor through Israel (Isa 44:23; 46:13).
   (2) All Israelites (the entire remnant) are included in this shoot planted by God, and thus will be Godly and display His splendor (Isa 60:21).
   (3) At the designated time, God will swiftly accomplish this transformation in His people (Isa 60:21-22).
   (4) The result will be that righteousness, which evokes praise to God, will spring up in view of all the nations (Isa 61:11).

   d. **PROMISES associated with the planting**: God's future purpose for His special peoples' fruitfulness is guaranteed to be fulfilled in **a series of everlasting covenants** pertaining to Israel during the Millennial Kingdom.
   (1) Chief among these promises of God is the **NEW COVENANT** guaranteeing them spiritual life (salvation from sin and regeneration). "'**I will make a new agreement with the whole nation of Israel after I plant them back in the land,' says the Lord.**" (v. 33 of Jer 31:31-34 NET).

- (a) **Inward Renewal**: His law will illuminate and dominate their minds and inward being, resulting in a personal relationship with Himself [(v. 33) Clarified in e, Power to Assure Success].
- (b) Pardon of sins and iniquities
  - God's anger replaced by salvation (Isa 12:1-3).
  - Their sins forgiven and forgotten (Jer 31:34; 33:8; 50:20; Isa 33:24).
  - Their disgrace removed (Isa 25:8).
  - Their shame forgotten (Isa 54:4; Ezek 39:26).
  - Their lives purified (Ezek 36:25; 37:23).
  - Their crippled condition healed (Micah 4:6, 7).

(2) **Additional covenants** bearing promises of God for Israel during the Millennial phase of the Kingdom and beyond. Though these are listed under several different scriptural references, no attempt is made herein to distinguish these stated agreements of God from one another or provide any specific nomenclature to them. The following is merely **a partial listing of promises included in or related to such affirmations of God concerning His proposed benevolence to Israel.**
  - (a) Jer 32:40-41,42,44: "I will make **an everlasting covenant** with them."
    - "I will never stop doing them **good**."
    - "I will inspire them **to fear Me**, so they will never turn away from Me."
    - "I will rejoice in doing them good and **will assuredly plant them in this land with all my heart and soul**."
    - "I will give them all the **prosperity** I have promised them."
    - "I will **restore** their fortunes."
  - (b) Ezek 37:26-27 MLB: "I will make with them **a covenant of peace**; it shall be **an everlasting covenant**."
    - "I will bless them and multiply them."
    - "I will set my sanctuary (dwelling place) in the midst of them for all time."
    - I will be their God and they shall be my people."
  - (c) Isa 54:10 NET: "Even if the mountains are removed and the hills displaced, My devotion will not be removed from you, nor will **My covenant of peace** be displaced."
  - (d) Ezek 34:25 NET: "I will make **a covenant of peace** with them and will rid the land of wild beasts, so they can live securely in the wilderness and sleep in the woods."

e. **POWER to Assure Success of the Planting**—the viability of the planted shoot is assured by Israel's filling with the Holy Spirit (as promised in the New Covenant).
  (1) Israel's transformation from usefulness to fruitfulness will begin with the pouring upon them of the Spirit (Isa 32:15; 44:3; Ezek 36:26, 27; 39:29) Note the similarity to God's initiation of the Church on the Day of Pentecost (Acts 2:1-4).
  (2) As a result of the Spirit's filling **Israel will display God's splendor**
    - (a) They will have a complete change of heart and spirit, as evidenced by a desire and resolve to follow the Lord's decrees (Ezek 36:26, 27).
    - (b) Their lives will evidence the fruits of the Spirit (Isa 26:2; 60:21).
    - (c) "They will do no wrong" (Zeph 3:12, 13).
    - (d) They will be enabled to fulfill their assigned responsibilities (Isa 28:6).
  (3) As a result of the Spirit's filling, **Israel will personally know the God of Splendor** (Jer 31:33-34; 32:38, 39; Isa 44:3-5).

The Millennial Kingdom

(4) The Spirit will not only regenerate the people but bring about an amazing transformation of the land upon which they are planted (Isa 32:15-16).

Note: The transformation of the land is outlined in Section C, "The Center of the Kingdom."

f. PATRONAGE (God's personal participation on Israel's behalf) **will assure that His objectives for the planting are achieved** (Isa 60:21-22; 61:11).
   (1) **He will comfort them** by reversing their circumstances (Isa 61:3 MLB; Jer 31:25; Isa 12:1).
      (a) "the laurel wreath (of victory) instead of the ashes (of defeat),
      (b) the oil of joy instead of mourning,
      (c) the mantle of praise instead of the spirit of heaviness."

   Note: These transformations are directly linked in the context of Isa 61:3 to the Israelites becoming "Oaks of Righteousness."

   (2) **He will clothe them with a robe of righteousness** (Isa 61:10).
   (3) **He will shower them with innumerable blessings** (Ezek 34:26).
      (a) Blessed beyond their fondest dreams and expectations (Psa 126:1-3; Isa 33:17; Zech 8:6).
      (b) Blessed beyond 100% (Isa 61:7; Zech 9:12).
      (c) Blessed beyond a normal lifetime (Isa 65:22).
      (d) Blessed beyond the first generation–to all succeeding generations within the 1,000 year period (Isa 61:9; 65:23; Jer 32:39).
      (e) Blessed beyond the Millennium "…an everlasting covenant".
      (f) Blessed inside and out (Enumerated in g, "Prosperity of the Planted Shoot").
      (g) Blessed conspicuously–recognized by the nations as those whom the Lord has blessed (Isa 61:9).
      (h) Blessed continuously–"I will never stop doing good to them" (Jer 32:40).
   (4) **He will shepherd them**–"He will watch over His people like a shepherd watches over His flock" (Jer 31:10 NET; Ezek 34:31).
      (a) **Provision**: Feeding them in rich pastures (Ezek 34:13-14, 29).
      (b) **Persistent attention to** their individual **needs**–"I will seek the lost and bring back the strayed; I will bind up the wounded; I will strengthen the sick…" (Ezek 34:16 MLB).
      (c) **Protection**: The security of His flock will concern the Shepherd (Micah 5:4-5). He will provide them security in: their homes (Isa 32:28), nature (Ezek 34:25, 28), agriculture (Ezek 34:27), and human relationships (Ezek 34:28).

g. PROSPERITY of the Planted Shoot–"I will make prosperity your overseer" (Isa 60:17 NET).
   (1) **Prosperity promised** in God's affirmations concerning Israel (Jer 32:40-42). Israel to receive "**a double portion**" (Isa 61:7).
   (2) **Prosperity realized internally: their souls become "like well watered gardens"** (Jer 31:12, 13).
      (a) Clean Souls–all impurities washed away (Ezek 36:25; 37:23).
      (b) Oriented Souls–led by the Lord (Isa 30:21).
      (c) Educated Souls–responsive to the Lord (Isa 29:24; Ezek 36:27).

- **(d)** Occupied Souls–enlisted and empowered to serve Him (Isa 28:6).
- **(e)** Peaceful Souls–the product of righteousness (Isa 32:17).
- **(f)** Joyful Souls–(described in (6)(b), page 89).
- **(g)** Enriched Souls–"He will be… a rich treasure of salvation, wisdom and knowledge" (Isa 33:6); "a crown of glory… to His people" (Isa 28:5 MLB).

(3) Prosperity Experienced and Viewed Externally

- **(a)** In **Jerusalem**: "I am ready to extend to her prosperity that will flow like a river…" (Isa 66:12 NET; Jer 33:9).
- **(b)** In **Agricultural productivity**
  - Success is guaranteed, from seed to satisfaction at the dinner table, from planting to partaking (Amos 9:14; Isa 30:23).
  - No crop failures (Ezek 34:27).
  - No crop losses to enemies (Isa 62:8-9).
  - Double cropping (i.e. year-round production–Amos 9:13).
  - Bumper crops in a diverse agriculture (Jer 31:12).
  - Even the beasts of burden dine on delicacies (Isa 30:24).

  Note: The environmental elements constituting and contributing to such superior productivity, approaching that of Eden, are outlined in Section C.

- **(c)** In the accumulation of the **wealth of nations** (Isa 60:5, 11, 16-17; Isa 66:12). "…and with their **riches you shall become famous**" (Isa 61:6 MLB).
- **(d) In security**. "My people will live in peaceful settlements, in secure homes, in safe quiet places" (Isa 32:18 NET).
  - "None of them will turn up missing" (Jer 23:4 NET).
  - No one will make them afraid (Ezek 34:28 NET).
- **(e) In peace**
  - As promised in His covenants (enumerated in Section 3d on pg. 86).
  - Affecting all aspects and relationships of their lives (Isa 11:13; Ezek 34:25; Micah 4:4).
  - Abundant (Jer 33:6).
  - Awesome (Jer 33:9).
  - Prevailing (Psa 72:7).
- **(f)** In **robust physical health and long life** (Isa 65:20, 22). "No resident of Zion will say 'I am ill'" (Isa 33:24 NET).
- **(g) In progeny**:
  - Numerically multiplied (Isa 27:6; Jer 23:3; 33:22).
  - These future generations will also enjoy spiritual and physical prosperity (Isa 54:13).

(4) The Purpose of Prosperity: To bring about a true appreciation of God in the hearts and minds of mankind:

- **(a)** All men (**Isa 41:20**), both
- **(b)** Israel (Isa 29:23) and,
- **(c)** The nations (Isa 61:9; Psa 126:2).

Note: Such appreciation of God is directly related to His overall objectives during Christ's Millennial reign. This subject will be considered more extensively in Section 4, "Fruition in the Land."

- (5) **The Timing of Prosperity**: To begin shortly after the devastation of Armageddon (Isa 30:25), and continue for the entire 1,000 years (Ezek 38:10-12).
- (6) **The Response to Prosperity**–Includes both **Thanksgiving** and **Joy** (Isa 51:3).
  - (a) **Thanksgiving**: Credit given where credit due: "O Lord, …all we have accomplished, **you have done for us**" (Isa 26:12). They will wear "a garment of praise instead of a spirit of despair" (Isa 61:3).
  - (b) **Joy**: Israel's mourning is destined to be replaced forever with "**the oil of gladness**" (Isa 61:3; Jer 31:13).
    - This joy begins on the day they set foot back in the land (Isa 35:10; 51:11).
    - It progresses during the 1,000 years as they proceed to rejoice in:
      - The King's provision of salvation and righteousness (Isa 61:10).
      - The King's righteous judgments (Psa 48:10, 11).
      - The restoration and productivity of the land (Jer 31:12; Joel 2:22-24).
      - The fruits of their labors (Isa 65:21-22).
      - The prosperity and peace of Jerusalem (Isa 66:10-14; Psa 132:13-16).
      - The restoration of their fortunes (Psa 53:6).
      - The wealth God showers upon them (Isa 60:5-9).
      - The double portion they will be receiving (Isa 61:7).
    - It continues for all eternity (Isa 61:7).

h. **PERMANENCE of the Planting**
- (1) Permanent Viability Guaranteed (Jer 32:40).
  - (a) God will **continually** be their benefactor
  - (b) Israel will **continually** revere God
- (2) Permanent Protection Afforded–"…they shall never again be uprooted" (Amos 9:15).
- (3) Permanent is Defined as "Everlasting"–The planting is the product of an everlasting covenant (Jer 32:40, 41; Ezek 37:26-28).

4. **FRUITION IN THE LAND**

a. **The Goal**: As previously stated, God's objective in planting Israel in their land will be that He might be glorified (Isa 61:3), both in them and through them to the nations. From the creation, a primary objective of the Lord has been: "Let the whole earth fear the Lord! Let all who live in the world stand in awe of Him" (Psa 33:8 NET). During the Millennial Kingdom He will accomplish this objective; He will expose His glory to all mankind; He will set the record straight as to who He really is. Indeed such revelation of Himself to the world may well be the primary purpose of this climactic period of history. This purpose could be divided into **two major objectives**.

(1) **Objective #1: The intimate revelation of Himself to Israel**–"My people will know My Name, …they will know at that time that I am He who says, 'Here I am.'" (Isa 52:6 NET).

"After I plant them in the land, …I will be their God and they shall be My people…**all of them, from the least to the most important, will know Me.**"

—Jer 31:33-34 NET

(2) **Objective #2: The revelation of His Holiness and Glory through His people to the nations**. (Correcting all previous misconceptions).

"I will make known My Holy Name among My people Israel...**and all the nations will know that I the Lord am the Holy One of Israel.**"

—Ezek 39:7

"**I will show Myself Holy through them in the sight of many nations.**"

—Ezek 39:27 (see also Ezek 37:27, 28)

Note: The above passages make it abundantly clear that the perception of God's holiness by the nations is directly linked to the distinctive work He will accomplish within and on behalf of Israel; the nations will observe the glory of the Lord as it bounces off Israel and is reflected to them. The very things Israel will experience as the **shared glory** of God, the nations will perceive as His **revealed glory**. As Israel stands with the Lord in the arena of a separated life and actually assimilates God's glory (through the Spirit), the nations will observe His glory from their cheering section in the bleachers.

> It should also be noted that God's restoration and exaltation of His people will not be something that they have earned or deserve. Neither will their welfare be the Lord's primary motive for accomplishing such a transformation.–Rather, it will be done to demonstrate His own holiness, and erase the former profaned image of Himself that Israel was responsible for projecting (Ezek 36:22, 23, 32).

  b. **The First Objective Achieved**–"At that time the Lord of Hosts will become a beautiful crown and a splendid diadem for the remnant of His people" (Isa 28:5 NET).
   (1) Israel's initial recognition that He is indeed **the Lord their God** seems to be associated with their realization that He has bestowed upon them both His justice and mercy; first sending them into exile for their transgressions and rebellion, and then cleansing and restoring them politically, physically, and spiritually (Ezek 39:28-29).
   (2) The continued revelation of Himself to Israel will be **made possible through His relationship with them.**
      (a) Personally living among them (Ezek 37:27-28).
      (b) Personally living within them (Ezek 39:29).
   (3) The revelation of Himself to Israel will be **accomplished primarily through His ministry in them** (internal changes).
      (a) They will perceive **His Righteousness** when He purifies their hearts (Ezek 37:23).
      (b) They will perceive **His Grace and Forgiveness** when He vanquishes from their memory every detail of their former iniquity (Jer 33:8; 50:20).
      (c) They will realize **His Peace** as He refreshes their souls (Jer 31:25).
      (d) they will appropriate **His Wisdom and Knowledge** as He opens their minds and hearts to receive His instruction (Isa 29:24; 33:6).
      (e) They will mirror all of **His Attributes** as the Spirit of God bears His fruit in their lives. Recognized as "the Holy People" (Isa 62:12).
   (4) The progressive revelation of Himself to Israel will be **accomplished secondarily through His ministry on their behalf**–external works and blessings.
      (a) Israel will recognize that **He is the Lord their God** when He displays His glory through His judgments at Armageddon (Ezek 39:21, 22).
      (b) They will experience **His Power** when He raises them from the dead (Ezek 37:13, 14).

- **(c)** They will witness **His Love and Grace** when He reaches out to bring them home (Ezek 39:25).
- **(d)** They will view **His Majesty** as he resides in their midst (Isa 12:6).
- **(e)** They will note **His Providential Concern** as He "watches over them to build and to plant" (Jer 31:28). Their appreciation of **His Protection** of them will be magnified when they view their infant children playing unharmed near the hole of the Cobra; even placing their hand into the viper's nest without injurious consequences (Isa 11:8-9).
- **(f)** They will benefit from **His Goodness** as He persists in pouring blessings into their lives (Jer 32:40).
- **(g)** They will begin to appreciate **His Unfathomable Wealth** when His blessings to them exceed even a "double portion" (Isa 61:7).
- **(h)** they will marvel at **His Love** as He works on their behalf "with all My heart and with all My Soul" (Jer 32:41 MLB)–especially as they recall their own former failure to love and serve Him in this very way, as prescribed in His law.
- **(i)** They will exercise **His Joy** when they view the former deserts blooming like Eden (Isa 51:3; Jer 31:12-15).
- **(j)** They will be awed by **His Omnipotence, Omniscience, and Omnipresence** as He brings into righteous subjection the entire world.
- **(k)** When they have successively experienced His deliverance, restoration, revelation, and blessings, and understand that He is utilizing them to vindicate His holiness to the nations, they will know intimately and beyond any doubt that **He is the Lord their God** (Ezek 39:27-29).

(5) The revelation of the Lord to Israel will be acknowledged by His people.
- **(a)** A sequence of responses **(Isa 12:1-6)**.
  - **Recognition** of His mercy and deliverance (v. 1-2), mighty acts (v. 4, 6), uniqueness (v. 4), magnificent accomplishments (v. 5).
  - **Trust** in the Lord (v. 2)–including honor and respect (Isa 29:23-24).
  - **Joy**–both within (v. 3) and externally expressed (v. 6).
  - **Praise** to the Lord (v. 4-5).
  - **Proclamation** to the world (v. 4-5).
- **(b)** The development of a proper response. "For as the ground produces its crops and a garden yields its produce, so the sovereign Lord will cause righteousness to grow, and give His people reason to praise Him in the sight of all the nations" (Isa 61:11 NET).

c. **The Second Objective Achieved**–the glory and holiness of God is conveyed to the nations as the Lord resides among a restored and regenerated Israel (Ezek 39:27).

(1) **The Transformation He will perform is stated by the Lord**: "I will sanctify My Great Name, that has been profaned among the nations, that you (Israel) have profaned among them. **The nations will know that I am the Lord,** declares the Sovereign Lord, **when I am sanctified among you in their sight**" (Ezek 36:23 NET).

Note: God will use the very agent most responsible for degrading and distorting the image of His character to demonstrate His perfect holiness.

(2) **Israel's Roles:**
- **(a) A passive object of God's benevolence**–one way God's identity is revealed to the nations is through His unsolicited acts on Israel's behalf–"All the nations will hear about

the good things I will do to them (Israel)…the nations will tremble in awe at all the peace and prosperity that I will provide for it" (Jerusalem) (Jer 33:9 NET; Mal 3:12). Judging from their subsequent comments, it is evident that the nations are carefully watching God's generosity on Israel's behalf–"At that time the nations said, '**the Lord has accomplished great things for these people**'" (Psa 126:2 NET).

The show goes on: "Their **descendents** will be known among the peoples (of the world). All who see them will recognize that **the Lord has blessed them**" (Isa 61:9 NET).

(b) An active participant in Godly living–the glory and holiness of God will be manifested through the lives of His people–"All your people will be godly, …they will be the product of My labor, **through whom I reveal My Splendor**" (Isa 60:21 NET; see also v. 1-3).

- The nations will observe Israel's distinct (separated) behavior and refer to them as "**The Holy People**" (Isa 62:2, 12; 61:10; 45:25).
- The nations will also observe Israel's every-growing praise of the Lord (Isa 61:11). (The overflow of a righteous, Spirit-filled life).

(c) A faithful proclaimer of God's glory and truth
- Chosen and recreated by God to be His witnesses, and to praise Him (Isa 43:10, 21).
- Obligated to share–"Tell the nations what He has done!" (Psa 9:11 NET).
- Provided with messages to publicize throughout the earth.
  - **Announce**: (Psa 96:10 NET)
    "The Lord reigns!
    "The world is established, it cannot be moved,
    "He judges the nations fairly."
  - **"Make it Known:"** (Isa 12:4-5 NET)
    "His acts are mighty!"
    "He is unique (holy)!"
    "He has done magnificent things!"
  - **"Tell about:"** (Psa 96:3-4 NET)
    "His splendor!…
    "His amazing deeds…
    His greatness–"awesome"
  - **Issue directives**: (Psa 96:7-9)
    "Ascribe to the Lord the glory due His name"
    "Worship the Lord in the splendor of His holiness"
    "Tremble before Him, all the earth."

(3) The Nations Perception of Christ and Response to Him
  (a) Recognition of various aspects of His holiness (Psa 97:6).
  - **Through His judgments** the people of the world will **learn righteousness** (Isa 26:9). Such enlightenment to the Lord's justice (Isa 51:4-5) will come as they observe the Royal Judge in action:
    - They will observe the King's just arbitration of international disputes (Isa 2:4).
    - They will discover that in all matters, great and small, the Lord rules peoples justly and guides the nations of the earth (Psa 67:4).

The Millennial Kingdom

> **Note:** As a result of recognizing the Lord's righteous judgments, they will come to the realization that He formerly punished and exiled Israel, the nation He loved, because of Her sins (Ezek 39:21-24).

- They will recognize Israel's salvation as a demonstration of **the Lord's love, grace, and faithfulness** (Psa 98:3). Formerly the nations had concluded that God had given up trying to restore this nation. This delusion was verbalized as follows: 'The Lord has rejected the two families of Israel and Judah" (Jer 33:24 NET). Israel had given them good reason to expect such rejection (II Kings 21:9).
- They will also recognize the **Lord's royal power** in His deliverance of Israel (Isa 52:10). Power sufficient to not only save Israel from her sinful condition, but to make her holy as He Himself is Holy. The latter fact will become evident when they observe that the Lord has actually established His permanent residence, and center of worship and government, in Israel's midst (Ezek 37:28).
- They will recognize **the standards of a Holy God** as they are communicated by the Lord from Jerusalem (Isa 2:3).
- "They will see **the glory of the Lord** and **the splendor of our God**" when they visit the Land of Israel and the Capital of the world (Isa 35:1-2; 2:2).
- Even foreigners (Psa 67:4) will participate in the **Joy of the Lord** as it spreads to distant lands (Psa 97:1). All the earth will be invited to join a world-wide praise choir in a celebration of joy (Psa 98:3-9). A special source of joy for the entire earth will be Jerusalem, the City of God. Partly because of its lofty position and exquisite beauty, but mostly because of the glory of its Royal Resident (Psa 48:1-2).

(b) Desire for greater understanding, compliance and acceptance as citizens of His Kingdom
- **Expressed in Repentance**
  - "At that time they shall call Jerusalem the throne of the Lord, and all nations will be gathered to it, in the name of the Lord; and they shall no more stubbornly follow their own evil heart" (Jer 3:17 MLB).
  - "From the ends of the earth," men come confessing their former ignorance and idolatry and seeking the truth (Jer 16:19-21).
- **Expressed in their dependence on the Lord**–When He gets their attention, the nations rally to the Lord (Isa 11:10).
  - "Many peoples and powerful nations will come to Jerusalem to seek the Lord Almighty and to entreat Him" (Zech 8:20-23).
  - Many people will also come to the Lord in Jerusalem, the center for moral instruction, to be personally taught **His standards and requirements**, intent on doing them (Isa 2:3).
- **Expressed in their dependence on Israel**
  - **For Enlightenment:** They come to Israel out of spiritual and moral darkness when they observe the bright light of God's splendor reflected from them (Isa 60:1-3).
  - **For Counseling and Comfort:** recognizing that "each man (among Israel's leaders) will be a shelter from the wind and a refuge from the storm, like streams of waters in the desert, and the shade of a great rock in a weary land" (Isa 32:2).

- **Expressed through their waiting** patiently and in anticipation **for the Lord** to demonstrate His power to deliver and establish them in righteousness (Isa 51:5).
- **Expressed through fulfillment of obligatory Worship of the Lord**–An annual pilgrimage (Zech 14:16-19; Isa 66:23)
- **Expressed through gifts and service** (Psa 72:10, 11; Isa 18:7).

d. The Goal Achieved: "...for the earth will be full of the knowledge of the lord, as the waters completely cover the sea" (Isa 11:9).

(1) All nations will recognize **His power to save, and His righteousness** (Psa 98:2; Isa 45:21-24).

(2) All nations will perceive **His greatness** (Micah 5:4).

(3) All nations and their leaders will respect and revere the character and glory of the Lord (Psa 102:15).

(4) All nations will honor, praise, and worship Him (Psa 86:9; 48:10; Isa 24:14-16).

(5) **Some from many nations** will join themselves to the Lord and become His people (Zech 2:11).

(a) Becoming truly repentant (Jer 3:17).

(b) Receiving a new birth (Psa 87:3-7).

C. THE CENTER OF THE KINGDOM

A Pearl of Great Price is placed into a setting that will enhance its beauty. Thus the abode of the King of Kings, during His millennial reign, as well as the homeland of the nation with whom He shares His glory and authority, will indeed be worthy of royalty. Physically, biologically, architecturally and aesthetically, the setting designed and formed by God for Israel's homeland, and the Capital of His worldwide Kingdom, will truly reflect the wisdom, glory, power and beauty of the Lord.

Glimpses of the grandeur and beneficial qualities of this handiwork of God, as well as less glamorous facts regarding the survey, division, restoration, occupation, and utilization of the land, are unveiled in Old Testament Scripture, and borrowed in part for the following portrayal of the Land of Israel and City of Zion, during this climatic era of world history.

1. **THE LAND OF ISRAEL**

a. **Its Political Prominence**–recognized by the nations as "The Center of the Earth" (Ezek 38:12 MLB).

b. **Its Priority in God's Program**–an essential ingredient in God's plans for His people–"He picked out for us a special land to be a source of pride for Jacob, whom He loves" (Psa 47:4 NET).

(1) Historically "His land and people" are inseparably woven together in His plans (Deut 32:43).

(2) At no time in history will this relationship be more apparent than during His millennial reign, when the land becomes **the inheritance** to which the Lord returns His people (Jer 16:15); **the field** in which He plants them (Amos 9:15); **the home** in which He establishes, satisfies, and refreshes them (Jer 31:24-25); and **the pasture** in which He shepherds them, providing both security and blessings (Ezek 34:23, 25-26).

(3) God's people are promised a double blessing: "**Your eyes will see the King in His beauty; they will behold a land that stretches far.**" (Isa 33:17 MLB).

The Millennial Kingdom

- c. **Its Perimeter Boundaries**
  - (1) The Lord dictated the survey specifications for Israel's millennial borders to the Prophet Ezekiel (Ezek 47:13-20).
  - (2) The boundary specified is very similar, perhaps identical, to that described to Moses for the division of the Land of Canaan (Num 34:1-12). It does not include the territory of Gilead on the east side of the Jordan, which Moses allotted to the tribes of Gad and Rueben, and half the tribe of Manasseh, upon their request (Num 32:5, 29, 33; 34:15).
  - (3) It is interesting to note that the route taken by the 12 spies, some 40 years prior to the Lord's first disclosure of the land's boundaries, passed through the very heart of God's eventual choice, from its southern extremity to its northern (Num 13:21-25).

- d. **Partition of the Land**–A plan drafted centuries prior to implementation (Ezek 47:21; 48:1-29).
  - (1) Unlike previous arrangements of tribal allotments, the land will be divided into 13 parallel horizontal bands, each completely crossing the land from its western boundary to its eastern, and tiered from north to south.
  - (2) One specific horizontal band will be allocated as **the Lord's portion**, and will cross the land at the latitude of Jerusalem, extending from the Mediterranean Sea in the west, to the banks of the Jordan River and Dead Sea in the east. For its entire length, this band will be approximately 8 1/3 miles (13,125 Kilometers) wide (N to S). Along this band, at the longitude of Jerusalem, will be an 8 1/3 mile square that will be set apart for a sacred allotment and the City of Jerusalem. After considering the distribution, occupation, and restoration of the entire land of Israel, we will focus upon the City of Zion that occupies this approximately 69 square mile area in the heart of Israel. Among the many facts about the world's capitol that will be presented, will be specific information on the location, setting, layout, size, subdivision, and accommodations of this area.
  - (3) Each of the remaining 12 east to west bands will be allotted to a specific tribe, but in a different distribution pattern than the tribes had previously been settled in the land under Moses and Joshua. The allotments for seven of the tribes (Dan, Asher, Naphtali, Manasseh, Ephraim, Rueben and Judah) will be stacked to the north of the Lord's portion, and the allocations for the remaining five tribes (Benjamin, Simeon, Issacher, Zebulum, and Gad) will be tiered to its south. Each tribal portion will be equal in area, though varying somewhat in width (north to south) because of variance in the breadth of the land.

- e. **Possession of the Land**
  - (1) **A Brief History**:
    - (a) The Land of Canaan was given to Israel as a permanent inheritance (Gen 13:14, 15; 15:18-21; 17:8; Ex 6:8; 32:13; 33:1; Psa 105:8-11; 135:12).
    - (b) Procurement of the gift was delayed because of sin (Ezek 20:15-16).
    - (c) When procurement was finally initiated, the Lord directed that it be achieved by dispossessing the former inhabitants. To fail to drive them out would result in serious consequences (Num 33:50-53, 55, 56).
    - (d) "They came in and possessed it; but they did not obey Thy voice, or walk in Thy law; They did nothing of all Thou commandest them to do" (Jer 32:23 MLB).
    - (e) Israel failed to eradicate their predecessors as commanded. Instead they mixed with them and learned their ways, thus defiling themselves and polluting the land (Psa 106:34-39).
    - (f) 100% occupation was never achieved.

- **Not under Joshua**–though He allotted the Land according to the Lord's instructions through Moses (Josh 14:5), there were very obvious shortcomings in actual occupation of allotments (particularly along the Mediterranean coast, in the lands of the Philistines and Phoenicians, and in the north–the Lebanon Mountains, the Al Biqa Valley, the Anti Lebanon Mountains, and portions of the Syrian Desert).
- **Not under David or Solomon**–though the Kingdom was aggressively extended beyond Israel's designated borders under the leadership of King David, and economic control over additional territory was gained during Solomon's reign, the actual homeland deeded to Israel by God was never completely occupied.

(g) The enlarged but incomplete land was then portioned between Israel and Judah (I Kings 12:16-22), and in time neighboring nations began to chip away at its borders (Ezek 36:3).

(h) As a result of sin, Israel and Judah eventually lost their hold on the land (Jer 17:4; 32:23).
- First Israel (II Kings 17:6, 23).
- Then Judah (II Kings 24:1-4; 10-20; 25:1-12; 18-21).

Note: Even though exiled, the right of the descendants of Abraham to possess the land was never revoked. A permanent valid claim to their inheritance continues to exist to this day, based on God's covenant promises. See references listed under (a).

(i) In subsequent periods of history (between Old and New Testaments), various sized portions of the Land have been conquered and controlled by the Jews, but only temporarily. The most extensive of such occupations occurred near the end of 84 years of conquests by the Macabees, shortly before 76 B.C.

(j) Since 1948, Israel has resettled in what amounts to roughly ½ of the promised land, and exercises precarious control over an additional 1/5 of the whole (the West Bank)–[These estimates are only rough approximations.]

(2) Repossession and Occupation of the Whole of the Land by Israel will be Successfully Concluded during the Millennium (Isa 26:15; Jer 33:14; Ezek 20:42).

(a) Possession initiated by God–"For God will deliver Zion and build the cities of Judah; that people may dwell there and possess it." (Psa 69:35 MLB).

(b) Residence acquired by:
- Approved homeowners–"The offspring of His servants shall inherit it, and **they who love His name shall abide in it**." (Psa 69:36 MLB).
- Aliens–who by God's grace will receive an equal inheritance (Ezek 47:22-23).

(c) Occupation proceeds by:
- Tribe (Ezek 48:1-7, 23-29).
- Vocation–the people distributed in both rural and urban settings according to their occupational gifts and calling (Jer 31:24). Both cities and flocks are located in combination throughout the entire land (Jer 33:12-13).

(d) Possession is consummated through redemptive purchases (at least by some). Throughout the Land, real estate transactions will be consummated and deeds secured to upscaled property formerly evaluated as "desolate" and "waste" (Jer 32:15, 42-44).

Note: Jeremiah obediently purchases the deed to a worthless field he had inherited in his native land of Benjamin, thus publicizing and evidencing long term faith in God's promise to eventually restore the Land (Jer 32:6-15).

The Millennial Kingdom

- **(e) Perpetual Possession is insured by God's promises:**
  - To never be uprooted again (Amos 9:15).
  - To live there with their descendants forever (Ezek 37:21, 25).

f. Preparation of the Land for Occupancy and Utilization

(1) Recovery Required from the scars of past judgments and Gentile occupations—"…the devastations of many generations" (Isa 61:4 MLB; Amos 9:11).

- **(a)** The land, from ancient times, was assessed as "desolate" and "waste"–much of it void of inhabitants, man, or beast (Jer 32:43; 33:10, 12).
- **(b)** Things only get worse in the Day of the Lord (Lk 21:24).
- **(c)** By the time the remnant are brought home, their land will have become "a perpetual wilderness" (Ezek 38:8 MLB).

(2) Restoration Promised

- **(a)** In time to produce sustenance for His people at their homecoming (Ezek 36:8-11, 33, 34).
- **(b)** To reach the level of former fortunes (Jer 32:44; 33:10-13).
- **(c)** To proceed to a higher level of beauty and prosperity–"Certainly the Lord will console Zion, He will console all her ruins. He will make her desert like Eden, her wilderness like the Garden of the Lord" (Isa 51:3 NET). "And make you (the land) prosper more than before" (Ezek 36:11).
- **(d)** To share the worth of God Himself–"No longer shall your land be called desolate… your land shall be called 'Beulah'…your land married to Him" (Isa 62:4 MLB).

(3) Restoration Undertaken and Achieved

- **(a) Renovation By God**–"For God will deliver Zion and rebuild the cities of Judah that people may dwell there and possess it" (Psa 69:35 MLB).
  - **Christ** (the King) will fulfill God's covenant pledge by rebuilding the land and reassigning inheritances in it that were formerly desolate (Isa 49:8).
  - **The Holy Spirit** will perform supernatural transformations of the Land (as well as the people). A desolate land is transfigured at the same time that new life is poured out upon Israel from heaven (Isa 32:15). (Some of the Holy Spirit's physical and biological achievements are identified in Section (4) to follow).
  - It will become apparent that it is **the Lord** that has "rebuilt what was destroyed, and replanted what was desolate" (Ezek 36:36).
- **(b) Reconstruction By Human Agents**–"They will rebuild the perpetual ruins and restore the places that were desolate; they will reestablish the ruined cities, the places that have been desolate since ancient times " (Isa 61:4).
  - The role of the Israelites in initial cleansing of the Land is already included in the outline under post-Armageddon activities on page 73).
  - They will construct permanent homes for themselves (Isa 65:21-22).
  - They will replant the Land to multiple crops (Amos 9:14; Ezek 36:8-9).
  - They will be assisted in reconstruction by foreigners, volunteer assistants as well as bond-servants (Isa 60:10, 12; 14:1, 2). Aliens will also serve the Israelites in agricultural occupations (Isa 61:5).

(4) Restoration of the Land to Productivity and Beauty is Made Possible by a Transformed Environment–Advance site modifications are accomplished by God prior to any undertakings by men. He will bring about awesome changes in the landscape, climate, and natural resources of the Land; Thus setting the stage for the productivity, prosperity and peace which will characterize the next 1000 years.

- **(a) A Favorable Climate**
  - "Showers of Blessing"–rain is assured at appropriate times and seasons (Ezek 34:26; Isa 30:23).
  - Light is magnified and sustained (Isa 30:26).

  Note: The condition described in the above passage may be limited to an initial period when special needs, including accelerated photosynthesis, need to be met.

- **(b) An Awesome Hydrology**
  - An abundant water supply–"On every high mountain and every high hill there will be streams flowing with water…" (Isa 30:25 NET).
  - Even where least expected (Isa 35:6-7; 41:18; 43:20; 44:3).
  - The most outstanding and beneficial of all Israel's streams will be a river which has its origin in the heart of Jerusalem. This river and its miraculous hydrology and productivity are described in part 2, "The Capitol of the Kingdom."

- **(c) Productive Soils**
  - "I will establish for them a renown planting place…" (Ezek 34:29 NET).
  - Former desert soils will sustain deep rooted perennial tree crops (Isa 41:19) with new elevated levels of productive capacity (Isa 32:15).

- **(d) Total transformation of the vegetative landscape**
  - To support flocks throughout the land (Jer 33:12, 13).
  - To produce "vegetation renowned for its growth" (Ezek 34:29 MLB).
  - To exhibit remarkable vegetative diversity (Isa 41:19).
  - To reflect the very splendor of God (Isa 35:1, 2).

- **(e) The primary reason for such marvelous transformations: "I will do this so people will observe and recognize, so they will pay attention and understand that the Lord's power has accomplished this, and that the Sovereign King of Israel has brought it into being"** (Isa 41:20 NET). This is truly a unique reason for landscaping!

(5) Restoration Realized: Evidence of this success is presented in prior sections of the outline, particularly under: "Prosperity Experienced and Viewed Externally," located on page 88.

2. The Capitol of the Kingdom–Zion (Jerusalem)

Background: Zion was originally the name of a Jebusite fortress located on a prominent hill within the perimeter of what became the City of Jerusalem. King David conquered Zion, made the fortress his residence and renamed it: "The City of David." (II Samuel 5:6-9). He then initiated the expansion of the city (vs. 9), and eventually Jerusalem occupied a complex of several related hills or mounds, as well as intermediate saddles and swales. During this expansion, Solomon built the temple on Mt. Moriah (II Chron 3:1, 2), and arranged for the ark of the covenant and other articles of worship to be transferred from the original Zion (the City of David) to this nearby temple mount. From approximately that time, Mt. Moriah began to be called Mt. Zion or Zion (Psa 20:2). Eventually this title became a synonym for the entire city of Jerusalem (Isa 2:3; 4:3; 33:20).

During the Millennium, the general location of Zion (Jerusalem) will be similar, but its size, shape, and arrangement will change to meet God's specifications [identified in section b(4)], and its

The Millennial Kingdom

elevation will be much more pronounced in order to exhibit the greater glory of the King of kings who resides there, and make it a focal point for the entire world [see section b(3)].

a. **Jerusalem Loved by the Lord**–The Creator of heaven and earth has a special and deep affection for Jerusalem (Psa 87:1-3).
   (1) **An affection that resulted in a choice:**
      (a) "For the Lord has chosen Zion, **He has desired it for His dwelling**: 'This is My resting place for ever and ever; here I will sit enthroned for I have desired it'" (Psa 132:13-14). What an amazing thing! God, who created the entire universe, has chosen a site among men as His permanent residence.
      (b) "In this house and in Jerusalem, which I have selected out of all the tribes of Israel, **I will put My Name forever**" (II Kings 21:7 MLB, 4; II Chron 6:6)

      Note: Prior to the building of the temple, the Lord had already taken up permanent residence in Jerusalem (I Chron 23:25), thus He is there today, represented by the Spirit of God.

   (2) **An affection that has persisted through hard times:** Despite the fact that the Lord's personal relationship with the city's inhabitants was broken, and the city suffered numerous devastations and prolonged periods of occupation and degradation…
      The Lord has never forgotten her: "I have graven you upon the palms of My hands. Your walls are continually before Me" (Isa 49:14-16 MLB).
      The Lord has never forsaken her: "…and you Jerusalem shall be called 'Sought out; a city not forsaken'" (Isa 62:12 MLB).

      Note: God's chief concern is for the inhabitants of Jerusalem, His people, but in numerous passages He links Israel's welfare with that of the city He appointed for their contact with and worship of Himself. The people and city are uniquely bonded in God's thoughts, as expressed in His Word–so much so that it is difficult at times to separate the two (Isa 49:17-21; 40:1-2 and numerous other passages).

   (3) **An affection that was displayed by Christ during His incarnation** (Lk 19:41-44).
   (4) **An affection so great that Christ cannot rest or cease to intercede on Jerusalem's behalf** until salvation and righteousness radiate brightly from her (Isa 62:1).
   (5) **An affection that recruits servants of God to intercede for her establishment** (Isa 62:6-7)–especially those who share His love and compassion for Jerusalem (Psa 102:14).
   (6) **An affection that will be demonstrated in merciful restoration of the City**, at His set time (Psa 102:13, 16).
   (7) **An affection that will become particularly obvious during the Millennium.**
      "At that time, Jerusalem will become 'a crown of glory in the hand of the Lord, and a royal diadem in the palm of your God…you (Jerusalem) shall be called **My delight is in her**'" (Isa 62:3-4 MLB).

b. **Jerusalem Rebuilt by the Lord:** "…He shall rebuild My City…" (Isa 45:13 MLB).

   Note: The Lord's work will not be merely renovation or face lifting; nor will it be a salvage operation utilizing materials from former ruins (Isa 32:14); nor will He model it after historical renditions of the city and its structures. According to His own words, He will "**create**" a brand new Jerusalem (Isa 65:18), as unique a work as His creation of the heavens and the earth, both past and future.

(1) Purpose of the Reconstruction Expressed:
- **(a)** To be His desired, cherished, and perpetual **abode** (Psa 132:13-14).

    Note: Even three ancient Persian Kings recognized that the God who empowered them to rule had selected Jerusalem as his earthly residence (Ezra 1:2; 6:12; 7:15).

- **(b)** To provide a **temple-palace** where He will reign as both King and Priest (Zech 6:12-13).
- **(c)** To be a **source of joy** to His people and Himself (Isa 65:18-19).
- **(d)** To be "the **praise** of the earth" (Isa 62:7) unparalleled in beauty (Isa 54:11, 12).
- **(e)** To appear therein in His **glory** (Psa 102:16).

(2) A Site Chosen:
- **(a)** On the site of ancient Jerusalem, but with an enlarged perimeter (Jer 31:38-40).

    Note: This promise of a rebuilt city on the former site is given by the Lord in conjunction with His promise to Israel of a New Covenant (Jer 31:31-34).

- **(b)** The City's specific location in the Millennial version of the land of Israel: In the middle of a special allotment of land which Israel will dedicate to God for special uses (Ezek 48:8). This allotment occurs as a band of land 8 1/3 miles wide (N. to S.), which completely crosses the land at approximately the latitude of Jerusalem (For clarity refer back to "Partition of the Land" on page 95).

(3) A Foundation Provided
- **(a)** The Lord will place His city on the firm foundation of a mountain summit: "**It shall be in the latter days that the mountain of the Lord's house shall be firmly established as the highest of mountains** and be raised above the hills…" (Isa 2:2 MLB; Micah 4:1)

    Note: The establishment of this mountain is foretold verbatim in both Isaiah's vision concerning Judah and Jerusalem, and Micah's vision concerning Samaria and Jerusalem.

- **(b)** To accomplish this, the Lord will do some preliminary site prep:
    - He will transform hilly portions of central Israel, formerly referred to as "the mountains of Judah," into a level plain, or more likely an elevated plateau (Zech 14:10).

    Note: Some of this leveling may occur during the Day of the Lord when an earthquake judgment brings down mountains worldwide (Rev 16:20).

    - Then He will continue His resculpturing of the landscape by raising up and stabilizing the mountain supporting the City of Jerusalem (Zech 14:10).

- **(c)** The lofty stature of Mt. Zion will be awesome to behold:
    - Appreciated by men: "**Beautiful for elevation, the joy of all the earth is Mt. Zion,…the City of the Great King**" (Psa 48:2 MLB).
    - Envied by mountains: "The mountains of Basham are majestic mountains, rugged are the mountains of Basham. Why gaze in envy, O rugged mountains, at the mountain where God chooses to reign, where the Lord himself will dwell forever?" (Psa 68:15-16). (envied for both its majestic elevation and its royal occupant).
    - Referred to as "Chief among the mountains" (Isa 2:2).

(4) The City Laid Out

According to the plan conveyed to the Prophet Ezekial, an allotment 8 1/3 miles square will be reserved as the site of greater Jerusalem (Ezek 48:20). This 69 sq. mile site will be divided into three principle districts as follows:

(a) The district "set apart to the Lord;" "the Holy District"

Occupying an area 8 1/3 miles (E. to W.) x 3 1/3 miles (N. to S.) (Ezek 45:1; 48:9).

- The focal point of the Holy District will be the temple which will occupy a central position of ~ 18.5 acres (Ezek 45:2).
- Most of this Holy District will be occupied by the residences of the specially qualified Priests (the offspring of faithful Zadok), who will serve the Lord in His temple (Ezek 48:10-12). The unique relationship of the priests to this District is stated by God: "It will be a holy section of the Land, **it will be for the priests**…" (Ezek 45:4 MLB). Though the priests are privileged to enjoy homes adjacent to the temple, this real estate is not theirs as a permanent possession or inheritance. In fact, they will have no inheritance given them in the Land, because their relationship with the Lord is to be such that **He is their possession and inheritance** (Ezek 44:28).
- The Holy District will occupy a central position in greater Jerusalem, bordering both the District of the Levites (Ezek 48:12-13) and the District for common use (the City of Jerusalem proper). The City is probably on its south side (Ezek 40:2) and the District of the Levites to its north.

(b) The District of the Levites: An allotment of equal size and dimensions to the Holy District (Ezek 45:5; 48:13).

- Set apart for the Levites who maintain the temple and are responsible for the daily tasks and services performed there that are distinct from direct ministry and access to the Lord (Ezek 44:11, 13, 14).
- This district will contain numerous residential areas for the homes of the Levites (Ezek 45:5).
- The Lord considers the District of the Levites, along with the Holy District, to be consecrated to Himself. Therefore the Levites are obligated to retain the integrity of its unique ownership and use (Ezek 48:14).

(c) The District for the common use of the city, including residences, pastureland, and cultivated farm land. A total area of 8 1/3 miles, E. to W. x 1 2/3 miles, N. to S. (13.8 sq. miles) (Ezek 48:15). **This district will be subdivided as follows**:

- **The City of Jerusalem proper**, occupying a central position 1 ½ miles square (~ 6 miles in circumference) (Ezek 48:16, 35).
  - Featuring 12 gates, 3 on each side, bearing the names of the tribes of Israel (Ezek 48:30-34).
  - Belonging to the whole house of Israel (Ezek 45:6).
  - Housing "workers" from every tribe of Israel (Ezek 48:19).
  - Renamed "The Lord is There" (Ezek 48:35).
- **Pastureland** for the flocks and herds of the City's citizens–a band 437 ½ ft. wide surrounding the city (Ezek 48:17). It appears that all the urban sites of Israel will be linked with surrounding pasture for livestock (Jer 33:12, 13).
- **Cultivated Gardens** (Cropland)–Utilized by the city's workers for producing their food supply–tracts of land to the east and west of the city and its pastureland, each 3 1/3 miles, E. to W., and 1 2/3 miles (N. to S.)–a total of ~ 11 sq. miles or ~ 7,040 acres (Ezek 48:18-19).

Note: Though the three districts described in the preceding sub sections constitute distinct entities with unique purposes, they are collectively identified as a single allotment of 8 1/3 miles square (69+ sq. miles) that must be set apart to the Lord in the Land of Israel (Ezek 48:20). It is my personal opinion that this entire allotment constitutes the unit of land identified as Jerusalem, Zion, Mt. Zion, City of God, etc. during the millennial era.

According to Ezek 43:7, the Lord, in all His glory, will occupy the throne room in His temple, within the Holy District, and dwell in the midst of the people of Israel forever. However the city centered in the common district, which lies about 1 2/3 miles south of the Holiest Place, will be renamed: "The Lord is There" (Ezek 48:35). This title would seem to suggest that the two areas are both integral parts of God's resident city. Many prophetic OT passages, including the following example, simply identify the City of Jerusalem and/or **Zion**, without distinction of Districts, as the Lord's sovereign residence and base of operations; "For Zion will be the center for moral instruction; the Lord will issue edicts from Jerusalem" (Isa 2:3 NET).

(5) The Crown Jewel of the Lord's Building Program will be the Temple: "Because of Your temple in Jerusalem, Kings will bring you **gifts**" (Psa 68:29).

  (a) The temple of the Lord will probably occupy the very summit of Mount Zion.
   - The mountain itself is actually referred to as "the Mountain of the Lord's House" (Isa 2:2 MLB).
   - For the visionary tour of the millennial temple, from which Ezekial produced a detailed description of it, the prophet was taken to the top of "a very high mountain" (Ezek 40:2).
   - "This is the law of the **temple**: the whole area surrounding **the mountain top** is most holy. Behold this is the law of the temple" (Ezek 43:12 NKJV).

  (b) The temple will be built personally by Christ: "Behold the man who's name is Branch! He shall branch out (sprout up) from His place and build the temple of the Lord. **He shall build the temple of the Lord**, and **He shall fill it with splendor**; He shall sit and **rule upon His throne**, and He shall **be Priest on His throne**, and a perfect union shall reign between the two offices" (Priest and King) (Zech 6:12-13 MLB).–Four good reasons for calling it **the Lord's House**.

  Note: It appears that the Lord will have already completed His temple (unassisted by men) prior to the return of the remnant, and will reign over the children of Israel from the moment of their arrival home (Micah 4:6-7). Thus, "They shall come and sing out their joy **on the height of Zion**, and beam with joy over the bounty of the Lord,…" (Jer 31:12 MLB).

  (c) The temple will be a masterpiece of architecture, including simplicity of design, elegance, beauty, and wonderful proportional balance of its parts with the whole (described in Ezek 40:1-42:20).

  (d) The temple will be beautifully adorned (Isa 60:13; Haggai 2:7-9).

  (e) The temple will be functional–providing a facility for the multifaceted ministry of the Lord, as well as service and worship on His behalf.
   - **A residence** for the Lord (Psa 132:13).
   - **A temple** for earth's High Priest (Zech 6:13).
   - **A palace** and throne room for the King of Kings (Psa 2:6; 132:14).

The Millennial Kingdom

- **A legislative hall** from which He will dispense international law (Isa 2:3).
- **A courtroom** in which the Chief Justice will settle international disputes (Isa 2:4).
- **A lecture hall** where He will teach foreign students His ways (Isa 2:3).
- **A command center** for the Lord of hosts (armies) (Psa 24:7, 8; 48:8).
- **A banquet hall** where He will nourish the nations (Isa 25:6).
- **A fountain** from which He will pour forth blessings (Psa 134:3).
- **A retreat** where He will rest (Isa 11:10).
- **A work place** in which to serve the Lord (Ezek 44:14).
- **A sanctuary** in which to minister to the Lord and worship Him (Ezek 44:15-16).
- **An alter** upon which to present sacrifices and offerings to the Lord (Ezek 43:13-27).
- **A quiet place** in which to reflect on the Lord's loyal love (Psa 48:9).

(f) **The temple will be holy**–separated to the Lord.
- To a large extent the entire greater Jerusalem area will be holy (Zech 8:3; 14:20-21; Joel 3:17).
- But a special degree of holiness will characterize the Temple of the Lord–"This is the law of the temple. The whole area surrounding the mountain top is **most holy**. Behold, this is the law of the temple" (Zech 43:12 NKJV).
  - A wall 10½ feet thick and 10½ feet high shall surround the temple, not for defense, but to delineate a clear boundary between what is common (secular) and what is holy (Ezek 42: 20).
  - The only people to approach and serve the Lord in the inner sanctuary, **the Most Holy Place**, are a specially separated priesthood with unique requirements of dress and conduct (Ezek 44:15-31).

(6) **The City will be Blessed with Refreshing Water Courses:**

The entire land of Israel will be well watered–"all the ravines of Judah will run with water" (Joel 3:18). However the most unique and glorious of its streams will flow from the summit of Mt. Zion: "There is a river whose streams make glad the City of God, the dwelling of the Most High" (Psa 46:4 MLB).

(a) **The origin of these streams**: A fountain (spring) beneath the Temple (Joel 3:18; Ezek 47:1). From this single source, streams flow both east and west (Zech 14:8). (Perhaps these two streams are considered arms or channels of the river (singular) spoken of in Psa 46:4).

Note: Mt. Zion will be the highest point of a crest that divides two large watersheds; the western one draining into the Mediterranean Sea, and the eastern one draining into the Dead Sea.

(b) **The miraculous volume of these streams**
- Ezekiel was led by an angel on a 1-mile tour of the eastern arm of the river, beginning at its temple source (Ezek 47:1-7).
  - The stream came out from under the SE portion of the Temple wall as a mere trickle.
  - At the 1/3 mile point, it had become an ankle deep creek.
  - At the 2/3 mile point, it was a knee deep stream.

- At the 1-mile point, it was a large river, too deep to cross on foot, requiring swimming.
- The west flowing arm of the river probably exhibits similar miraculous increases in volume.
- The flow of these streams within the city limits, for several miles both east and west of the temple, will be that of a large river. The distance from the temple to either the eastern or western city limits is over 4 miles. If the streams become large rivers within 1 mile, they would then maintain or increase such flow for the balance of their course through the city. Thus Scripture foretells: "**Rivers and wide streams will flow through it** (Jerusalem)" (Isa 33:21 NET).

(c) **The miraculous quality of these streams—"Everything will live wherever the river goes"** (Ezek 47:9 MLB).
  - **Providing life to the Sea**: The waters of the stream flowing east will enter the deep depression of the Jordan Valley (Ezek 47:8), and then flow into the Dead Sea. Upon entering the latter body of water, miraculous changes will occur:
    - The extremely saline waters of the Sea will be rendered fresh (Ezek 47:8).
    - Consequently the Dead Sea will swarm with aquatic life; supporting dense populations of many species of fish (equaling the productivity of the Mediterranean Sea), and resulting in a thriving fishing industry that will line the Sea's western shore for at least 2/3 of its length (Ezek 47:9-10).

    Note: Swamps and marshes on the perimeter of the Dead Sea, or at its southern end, will not receive the stream's waters, and will be retained as valuable sources of various salts (Ezek 47:11).

  - **Providing Life to the Land**:
    - On both sides of the river will grow all kinds of evergreen fruit trees that bear edible fruit every month, and whose leaves are valuable for medicinal purposes (Ezek 47:12). These orchards line the stream even at its humble beginnings (Ezek 47:7).
    - Some dry unproductive land, which formerly supported only drought-tolerant plants such as Acacia trees, will also be watered by the stream originating at the temple, and be restored to productivity (Joel 3:18).

    Note: The "Shittim" (Valley of Acacias) identified by Joel in the preceding reference, may refer to the ancient town of Shittim, which was situated along a tributary on the east side of the Jordan River, approximately 5 miles north of the Dead Sea. In that case, the extension of the Stream's waters to Shittim could possibly mean that this valley area will be inundated, and included within the formerly Dead Sea, as its depth and surface area increases and spreads north.

(d) **The Benefits of the Waters to the City of Jerusalem**
  - Aesthetically pleasing and emotionally uplifting: "…whose streams make glad the City of God…" (Psa 46:4).
  - Providing a plentiful supply of fruit year round from the streamside orchards (Ezek 47:7, 12).
  - Providing irrigation, with life-giving water, for the gardens and cropland of the city. The flow of the river in its largest proportions would parallel, and correspond almost

exactly in length, to the croplands in the southeastern and southwestern portions of the City (those farmed by the workers in the City District). Thus only short canals or ditches would be required to deliver the water to adjacent fields, only 1 2/3 miles away. Undoubtedly bumper crops will be produced from the life giving water.

- c. **Jerusalem Glorified by the Lord**: He will not only rebuild Jerusalem, but will then appear there in His Glory! (Psa 102:16).
  - **(1) The single most distinguishing characteristic of the City of Jerusalem will be the Lord's sovereign presence**—Thus the City will be referred to by various names that relate the City to its resident King: "The City of our God" (Psa 48:1, 8); "The City of the Great King" (Psa 48:2); "His Holy Mountain" (Psa 48:1); "The City of the Lord" (Isa 60:14); "Zion of the Holy One of Israel" (Isa 60:14); "The Throne of the Lord" (Jer 3:17); "**The Lord is There**" (Ezek 48:35), to name a few.
  - **(2)** Because of His presence, **Jerusalem will be blessed with His visible radiant glory**
    - **(a) Spectacular glory will mark every step of the Lord's initial entrance into His newly created City to take up residence**. The landscape becomes radiant with His glory as He approaches the City from the east, and when He reaches His destination within the inner sanctuary, His glory fills the entire temple (Ezek 43:1-5).

      Note: Ezekiel likened the appearance of the Lord's glory to that He had envisioned at the River Chebar (Ezek 1:26-29). The glory he witnessed on that occasion emanated from the Lord Himself; a fiery brightness that produced a surrounding halo of brilliant light, similar to that of a rainbow in the clouds following a shower.

    - **(b) His radiant glory will continue to be witnessed**:
      "Then shall the moon blush, and the sun be ashamed (at the inferiority of their light); for the Lord of Hosts shall be King on Mt. Zion, and **in Jerusalem His glory shall be before His elders**" (Isa 24:23 MLB).
    - **(c) His glory will brighten the entire City**, shining on His people and attracting the nations out of darkness to His light (Isa 60:1-3).

      Note: According to verses 19 and 20 of Isaiah 60, the glory of the Lord, spoken of in verses 1 through 3, will be a permanent source of illumination for His people, replacing the light provided by sun and moon. It appears the Lord is speaking of the light of His visible radiant glory. However, there is evidence in this chapter and its context that some statements may be allegorical; that God is actually picturing the spiritual splendor of Christ with which he will perpetually enlighten the inhabitants of Jerusalem; a glory that will then be reflected through them to the world. Rather than being dependent on other humans, or their own hearts, both of which fluctuate like the light of sun and moon, the Lord Himself, and His Holy Spirit, will continually enlighten them, producing in their lives the attributes that distinguish His own glory of character [clarified in section (3) which follows].

      Isaiah 60 MLB begins: "Arise, shine, for your light has arrived, and the glory of the Lord rises (shines) upon you." Immediately preceding this exhortation is a promise of God: "This is My covenant with them; says the Lord: "**My Spirit, who is upon you, and My Words, which I have put in your mouth**, will not depart from your mouth, nor from the mouths of your children, nor from the mouths of their descendents, from this time on and **forever** says the Lord" (Isa 59:21). Note also that immediately after God's affirmation that the Lord is their everlasting light and source of glory (Isa 60:19-20), He pronounces: "Then will **all your people be righteous**, and they will possess the land forever. They are the shoot I have planted, the work of My hands **for the display of My splendor** (glory)" (Isa 60:21). His people cannot shine or display his radiant glory, but they will display His spiritual attributes, including His righteousness. This splendor will then be detected by the nations, who will come out of darkness seeking to share such glory.

(3) Because of His presence, Jerusalem will be characterized by the Lord's glorious attributes; to such a degree that some of His attributes will even be used as synonyms for the name of the City.

    (a) "…I will dwell in the midst of Jerusalem. Then Jerusalem shall be called the **City of TRUTH**" (Zech 8:3 MLB).

    (b) The Lord will reestablish a credible system of justice in Jerusalem. "After that you will be called 'a **Stronghold of RIGHTEOUSNESS**, the Faithful City'" (Isa 1:26 MLB). "**He will fill Zion with justice and righteousness**" (Isa 33:5).

    (c) "…the mountain of the Lord Almighty will be called '**the Holy Mountain**'" (Zech 8:3).

    "Then you will know that I the Lord your God, dwell in Zion My Holy Hill. **Jerusalem will be HOLY**;…" (Joel 3:17; Obadiah 1:17).

- Free from people or influences foreign to God (Joel 3:17; Isa 52:1).
- Its entire population will be holy (separated to God) (Isa 4:3).
- The highway into the City will be holy (Isa 35:8-10).
- Even the family cooking pots will be holy (Zech 14:21)

    Note: Historically Jerusalem was and is presently referred to as the Holy City, but prior to the Lord's residence in the City, the conduct of the inhabitants has shown this title to be a misnomer.

    (d) "Under His rule…**Jerusalem will live in SECURITY**" (Jer 33:16 NET). Security is a blessing of God rather than an attribute, but the City's security bears evidence of **the Lord's Righteousness,** (v 16), **and of His Strength and Power**: "…in the City of **the Lord Almighty**, in the City of our God, **God makes her secure forever**" (Psa 48:8).

Note: Psalm 48, which focuses on millennial Jerusalem and its King, speaks briefly of the City's beauty, but primarily emphasizes its security; a security which is based on the Lord's ability to protect and deliver. Included in this Psalm is a guided tour around the City to check out its fortifications (vs. 12-13). On this walk, God's people are asked to count her towers, to take note of her defense walls, and to walk through, or view, her fortresses. What we observe, we are to pass on to succeeding generations. My personal opinion is that the message that observers will pass on is that such fortifications are **non existent!** The City requires no such defenses "**for God, our God is our defender forever**"! (vs. 14 NET). This is the conclusion our guide wants us to reach.

Psalm 48 also includes an example of how "God made Himself known as a defense" by delivering the City and its people from the attack of a large enemy force (vs. 3-8). In the concluding chapter of this study, Period IV, we will refer to this particular deliverance when we focus on the final attack of Satan.

The Millennial Kingdom

"We have a **Strong City**! The Lord's deliverance, like walls and a rampart, make it secure" (Isa 26:1 NET).

See also: Psa 46:5-7; Isa 11:9; Zeph 3:16-17.

Note: The blessing of security during the Millennium is very important to Israel, because both the people and their capitol have experienced centuries of insecurity.

- (e) The nations will tremble in awe at all the **PEACE** and **PROSPERITY** I will provide it (Jerusalem)" (Jer 33:6-9).
    - "I will extend peace to her like a river, and the wealth of the nations like a flooding stream" (Isa 66:12).
        - ⋏ Jerusalem will be recognized as "a peaceful settlement" (Isa 33:20 NET).
        - ⋏ Jerusalem will bulge with prosperity (Isa 60:11).
- (f) A City of Great **JOY** (Isa 66:10).
    - Created anew for the purpose of being a source of joy (Isa 65:18).
    - It will fulfill its purpose and become a source of joy to the whole earth (Psa 48:2).
    - It will bring the Lord fame for the joy that He will bring to Jerusalem (Jer 33:9).
- (4) Conclusion: When the Lord glorifies Jerusalem, **the City "will be a crown of splendor in the Lord's hand, a royal diadem in the hand of your God!"** (Isa 62:3).

d. Jerusalem Enjoyed by its Residents

Note: Described herein is the population living in the city proper (i.e. in the District for Common Use), priests and levites are not included. In many respects the character, life style, and experiences of these residents are similar to citizens living throughout Israel.

- (1) **Their background:**
    - (a) Chosen representatives of every tribe of Israel (Jer 3:14; Ezek 45:6).
    - (b) All have their sins forgiven (Isa 33:24).
    - (c) All know God in truth and righteousness (Zech 8:8).
- (2) **Their loyalty:**
    - (a) They love His name (Psa 69:35, 36).
    - (b) They revere Him (Jer 32:39-40).
- (3) **Their spiritual character:**
    - (a) Every person on the City register will be holy (separated to God) (Isa 4:3; 62:12).
    - (b) All residents will be righteous (Isa 60:21).
- (4) **Their welfare:**
    - (a) **Enjoyable accommodations:** peaceful, secure, restful homes (Isa 32:18).
    - (b) **Good health:**
        - Experiencing no illness (Isa 33:24)–a bad market for medical practitioners and the pharmaceutical industry.
        - Enjoying fullness of life from infancy to old age (Isa 65:20, 22).
            - ⋏ The city streets filled with playing children (Zech 8:5).
            - ⋏ The city streets (not convalescent homes) occupied by seniors living and enjoying a ripe old age (Zech 8:4).
    - (c) **Prosperous:**
        - Well provided for by the Lord (Psa 132:15).
        - The recipients of the riches of the nations (Isa 66:12); the city gates remain open 24 hours a day to accommodate the flow of gifts into the City (Isa 60:11).

      (d) Secure: (Zech 14:11). The reasons for Jerusalem's security already identified in Section c(3)(d), pg 106.
- **(5) Their vocation:** The residents are referred to as "**workers,**" a title seemingly common to all (Ezek 48:18, 19).

    Note: We are not told the various individual occupations of the city's residents but the inclusive title "worker" implies that they are all productively employed; this term probably also speaks of their industriousness. We do know that, in addition to other daily tasks, all able residents (workers) will share the responsibility of farming the city's croplands and gardens that produce their food supply (Ezek 48:19).

    Living in a city deluged with gifts from abroad, it would be easy for Jerusalem's residents to become dependent on others, and in fact plain lazy. However, God's blessings are not found in leisure but in labor (Prov 14:23). In a perfect environment, Adam was given responsibilities to accomplish through manual labor, as well as intellectual exercise. In the restored environment of the Millennial Kingdom, His people will also be occupied with worthy tasks, coupled with periodic rest, worship, and abundant compensation: "**My chosen ones will long enjoy the work of their hands. They will not toil in vain...**" (Isa 65:22-23).

- **(6) Their preoccupation: REJOICING**
  - **(a)** The changing of the guard:
    - Weeping and sorrow pull out of town (Isa 30:19; 65:19).
    - Fasting is replaced by joyful festivals (Zech 8:19).
    - Joy is publicly expressed in song (Psa 132:16).
  - **(b)** Rejoicing for good reasons:
    - Jerusalem will be created for the purpose of being a delight and its people a joy (Isa 65:18).
    - Its residents will be delighted in the City's overflowing abundance (Isa 66:10, 11), and its exquisite beauty (Isa 54:11, 12).
    - They will enjoy the work of their hands (Isa 65:22).
    - But most of all, their joy will be expressed over the greatness of the Lord who dwells in their midst (Isa 12:6).

e. **Jerusalem Focused On by the Nations**
- **(1) The nations listen to favorable reports about Jerusalem.**
  - **(a) Concerning the Lord's treatment of Israel:** "All the nations will hear about all the good things which I will do to them (Isarel), and **this City will bring Me fame, honor, and praise before them for the joy that I bring it**" (Jer 33:9 NET).
  - **(b) Concerning spiritual rebirth of some of their own people** which have taken place in Jerusalem: "**Glorious things are spoken of you, O City of God**" (Psa 87:3 NKJV). Read Psalm 87 in its entirely and note that the foreigners who have come to a true knowledge of the Lord are acknowledged by their countrymen as having the special status of being born (anew) in Jerusalem.
- **(2) The nations visit Jerusalem:** The City becomes a priority destination in travel plans worldwide—"and you shall be called **Sought Out**; a city not forsaken" (Isa 62:12 MLB). Purposes for Visits:
  - **(a)** To experience the light from which they have been deprived by darkness (Isa 60:1-3).
  - **(b)** To behold the glory of the City (Isa 62:2).
  - **(c)** To entreat and seek the Lord (Zech 8:20-22).

The Millennial Kingdom

- **(d)** To be instructed by Him and learn His ways (Micah 4:2; Isa 2:3).
- **(e)** To voluntarily worship and serve the Lord, in honor of His name (recognizing Him for who and what He truly is) (Psa 86:8-10; 102:21, 22). Foreigners who "love the name of the Lord" will be gathered, by the Lord, to God's Holy Mountain to experience the same privileges and joys as Israel's remnant (Isa 56: 6-8).
- **(f)** To fulfill obligatory worship (Zech 14:16, 17) and service, including the delivery of gifts for the temple (Isa 60:10-13; Psa 68:29).

(3) **The nations' impressions** of what they see and hear:
- **(a)** They respect the reputation (character) of the Lord, and revere Him because of His splendor (glory). (Psa 102:15-16; 48:10).
- **(b)** They admire the loftiness and grandeur of the City–it becomes a source of joy worldwide (Psa 48:2)
- **(c)** Some from all nations will respond in repentance and faith, taking on the name of the Lord (Jer 3:17; Zech 2:11; Psa 87:3-7).

Addenda to The Foregoing Outline of Period III

In the preceding section of the outline, some selected subject matter on the Millennial Kingdom was introduced and discussed. For our glimpse at that future period, I chose to focus attention primarily on the glory of the Lord, His special relationship with the people, land, and capitol of Israel, and to the fulfillment of His purpose of making Himself known to the gentile nations. The reader should realize that there are additional subjects that could, and perhaps should have been included, to help characterize His terminal Kingdom on the current earth. Some of these potential topics are recognized in the following list, accompanied by a few Scriptural references, and brief comments. These are subjects I have not adequately studied and do not feel competent to discuss, thus the remarks represent impressions and problems rather than conclusions; more questions than explanations.

(1) **The location of the Church in the Millennial Kingdom**–According to Rev 7:15-17, we have an inseparable relationship with our Lord. How this relationship will be maintained (i.e. how we will serve him day and night and receive His Shepherd's care) while the Lord resides in His temple in Jerusalem, remains a mystery to me, though I'm sure it will be a reality.

(2) **The make-up, structure, and function of the government the Lord will establish under His sovereign rule**–We know that when Christ establishes His eternal Kingdom, and assumes authority over all dominions under heaven, His saints will share certain authority under His sovereignty (Dan 7:22, 27). Specifically identified as receiving such honorary administrative or judicial positions are resurrected Jewish saints who will be martyred for their testimony for Jesus during the Day of the Lord (Rev 20:4).

There are also Old Testament forecasts of Israelites who will exercise governmental responsibilities during that future era. For example, Isa 1:26: "I will restore your (Israel's) judges as in days of old, your counselors as at the beginning. Afterward you will be called the 'City of Righteousness,' the Faithful City."

What about the Church? In Rev 5:9-10, we read that men purchased for God, with the blood of the Lamb, from every tribe, language, people and nation, will be appointed as a Kingdom and priests to serve Him, and **to reign on the earth**. II Timothy 2:12 also affirms that we shall reign with Him. In fact, we "will reign forever and ever" when we serve the Lord in the New Jerusalem, following the creation of a new heaven and a new earth (Rev 22:3-5). But what about exercising such a privilege during the Millennial Kingdom? Following Satan's imprisonment in the Abyss, John "saw thrones on which were seated **those** who had been given authority to judge" (Rev 20:4). The identity of **"those"** is not given, nor are they clearly distinguished from the Jewish martyrs who John also observed, but one common interpretation is that they are the Church. Implicit in reigning with Christ seems to be some responsibility for judging this world (Rev 2:26-28). Statements by Paul to the Corinthians allude to the fact that Christians will have judicial responsibilities for affairs of this world as well as beyond (judging angels) (I Cor 6:2-3).

(3) **The Spiritual, Economic, Political, and Social status of Gentile Nations during the Millennial Kingdom.**

Spiritual life: In preceding sections of the outline we were reminded that when the earth is filled with the knowledge of the glory of the Lord, His attributes will be readily recognized worldwide. Consequently, He will be respected and reverenced throughout the international community. The world's masses will make annual pilgrimages to Jerusalem to worship the Lord, and many foreigners will voluntarily seek His favor and desire to learn His ways. Some from every nation will come to genuine repentance and faith, and enter into an eternal living relationship with Christ.

In at least two nations besides Israel, it appears that large segments of the population are received into fellowship with the Lord. One of these nations is Egypt: "So **the Lord will make Himself known to the Egyptians**, and in that day **they will acknowledge the Lord**. They will worship Him with sacrifices and grain offerings; they will make vows to the Lord and keep them." An altar dedicated to the Lord will be constructed in the heart of Egypt, and a monument honoring Him will be constructed at its border with Israel. A similar relationship with the Lord will be entered into by Assyria, and these two nations, along with Israel, will form a unique triad of nations that represent what God considers "**a blessing on the earth**" (Isa 19:18-25).

Aside from these unique examples, we know very little about how the spiritual enlightenment of the world's masses will be translated into daily living. Surely relationships between individuals and nations, as well as standards of morality, will improve to some unknown degree. However, in the final analysis, when the 1000 years will come to an end, we discover that the majority of earth's residents have deceitful hearts and rebellious natures (Rev 20:7-8).

Economy: As Israel experiences 1000 years of continuous prosperity, how do the nations fare?

Because wars, armies, and defense spending are no more, and selfishness, corruption, and violence are minimized, we would expect greatly increased expenditures of time and money in productive pursuits. Consequently, the quality of living will probably be raised significantly worldwide and poverty eliminated.

The suitability of lands for specific natural resources and agricultural products will continue to vary regionally and nationally, but it appears that levels of production will be favorable enough to permit generous exports of specialty products, from both the land and sea (Isa 60:6-9). I find no evidence that lands outside Israel will be blessed with supernatural climates, soils, and waterways as she will be, and since Israel will also receive continual gifts from the nations (Isa 60:5-7, 16-17; 61:6), her wealth and standard of living will probably far exceed that of other nations. In his final act of folly, (See Period IV), Satan will use Israel's wealth as an enticement to provoke the nations to envy, covetousness, and attempted plunder (Ezek 38:10-13).

Politics: The form of government worldwide will be a monarchy (theocracy) headed by the King of kings. Under such a system, will there be any national autonomy? Several promises, concerning the respect and favor the nations will grant to Israel during the Millennium, link the nations with their kings (Isa 49:23; 60:3, 10-11; 62:2). Thus it appears that the gentile nations will have leaders (kings) that come from their respective populations, rather than governors directly representing the Lord. These kings, though in servitude to the Lord, will provide a degree of self-government. Though there will be no true democracies in the world, there will be great liberty and freedom to do what is right.

All disputes between nations will be arbitrated by the Lord (Isa 2:4).

Moral Standards: The combination of continual exposure to truth, and being completely insulated from Satan's lies, should definitely change peoples' ideas and life styles, and contribute to improved human relationships worldwide. As already pointed out, the nations will receive instruction on the Lord's ways and standards on visits to Jerusalem as well as in their homelands, as messages and messengers are regularly dispatched from Jerusalem (Isa 2:3; Psa 9:11). Recognizing the fact that many citizens in most lands will not personally know Christ, some opposition to the Lord's standards can be anticipated. However, the Scripture informs us that there will be a significant positive response to His Word: "…and all nations will gather in Jerusalem to honor the name of the Lord. **No longer will they follow the stubbornness of their evil hearts**" (Jer 3:17).

The nations will also learn righteousness as they see it displayed in His people (Isa 60:21), and as they experience His judgments (Isa 26:9). As the Lord's truth and righteousness are translated into daily living, the moral standards will be elevated worldwide. For the first time in modern history, the standards of all nations will be similar; every nation will be on the same page.

Social Status: The gentile peoples of the world, for the most part, will consider themselves in a social strata inferior to Israelites, primarily because of the Jews special relationship to God–the beneficiaries of His Spirit and blessings (Isa 49:23, 26b; 61:9), and the recipients of the titles: "Priests of God" and "Ministers of our God" (Isa 61:6). Though the Jews will treat foreigners and aliens respectfully and kindly, they will employ many of them as servants and be their supervisors (Isa 14:1-2; 61:5).

(4) Will the Lord bring compensatory judgments against those nations who, prior to the Millennium, mistreated and oppressed Israel?

During the Millennial Kingdom, the attitudes and the actions of the nations toward Israel will remarkably change, as I have attempted to portray in the outline. In fact, when God sets the record straight, the reproach of His people will be removed from the earth (Isa 25:8). Hatred and contempt will be replaced by respect and admiration when God bestows upon Israel the garment of righteousness, and puts them on international display.

But what about the past? Will nations be held accountable for their bitter attitudes and cruel actions against Israel? It appears they will! "In those days and at that time when I restore the fortunes of Judah and Jerusalem, I will gather all nations and bring them down to the Valley of Jehosaphat (The Lord Judges) and enter into judgment against them concerning My inheritance, My people Israel, for they scattered My people and traded boys for prostitutes; and sold girls for wine that they might drink" (Joel 3:1-3).

Through His prophets, God made it clear that He holds the nations accountable for the enmity and cruelty they displayed against Israel (Ezek 28:24-26; 36:6, 7), and will require retribution from some specific nations for such attitudes and actions (Isa 34:8, 9; Jer 50:28; 51:49; Ezek 25:1-7; 26:2-6; Joel 3:19).

The question is, when will these judgments be administered? Numerous judgments against individual nations, most of whom are Israel's neighbors in the Middle East and North Africa, are recorded in portions of Isaiah, Jeremiah, and Ezekiel (also the entire Book of Nahum is devoted to a single judgment against Ninevah). The majority of these prophetic judgments have already occurred in recorded history, and it appears that most of those still future will occur during the 7 year period known as the Day of the Lord. In reference to that period, it will be said: "The Lord has opened His arsenal, and brought out the weapons of wrath." This is the principal time when God will call

The Millennial Kingdom

the nations into accountability for all their sins (Isa 24; 13:9-13), including the blood of His saints, both Jew and gentile (Isa 26:21; Rev 16:6; 17:6 w/ 18:6).

A few compensatory judgments effecting specific enemy nations may be reserved for the time when Christ is actually reigning on the earth. An example of such a possibility is found in the twenty-fifth chapter of Isaiah. The chapter begins with acknowledgement and thanksgiving to the Lord of judgments He has already historically accomplished, in accordance with plans announced long ago. The passage proceeds to look forward to His accomplishments for His people and the nations when he rules on Mt. Zion. At that time, when He exercises His sovereignty to save and establish His people, the Scripture also records: "Moab will be trampled under Him." (vs. 10-12).

Another possible example is noted in the eleventh chapter of Isaiah. Recorded in this chapter is an account of the regathering and return to their land of the remnant of Judah and Israel. At that time, when the Spirit of God transforms their lives, it appears some will be dispatched on a short term military operation against neighboring nations who previously persecuted them: "They will swoop down on the slopes of Philistia to the west, together (Israel and Judah) will plunder the people to the east. They will lay hands on Edom and Moab, and the Ammonites will be subject to them" (Isa 11:14).

Confirmation of such initial aggression against Israel's perennial enemies would require more study of this subject than I am currently prepared to pursue. I find it quite difficult to clearly distinguish the timing of some of God's prophetic judgments against individual nations. If indeed military action is taken, it is probably confined to a relatively brief initial stage of the Millennial Kingdom, because the Lord will terminate all warring between nations, disband armies, and convert weapons of war into implements of peace (Isa 2:4; Micah 4:3).

Before leaving this subject, I would like to introduce an additional passage of Scripture which directly addresses the subject of how God will deal with wicked neighbors of Israel who have seized portions of Israel's earthly inheritance (land). According to Jer 12:14, the Lord will initially punish these nations for such action by "uprooting" them from their own domains. However, eventually He will extend His compassion to them and bring them back from exile to their home countries and personal properties. Following their restoration, the Lord will give them a choice of two options. If they learn the ways of His people (Israel), and acknowledge their allegiance to the Sovereign God, then they will be established among His people. "But if any nation does not listen (so respond) I will completely uproot and destroy it," declares the Lord. Considering the conditions laid down by God, the timing of the restoration of these neighbors to their own lands would seem to be during the Millennial reign of Christ. During that period, God's people will be truly worthy of modeling a quality of righteousness which other nations should copy.

(5) What will the world look like outside of Israel?

In section C of the preceding outline of Period III, we caught brief glimpses of the beauty and high quality of natural resources that will characterize Israel during the Millennial Kingdom. Does such a healthy and productive environment represent natural conditions throughout the world?

Though I cannot seem to see much of the world's landscape of that era through the window of His Word, I am reminded that a seven year period of wrath will immediately precede the initiation of the Kingdom. During that brief span, ruinous changes in the environment will occur as a consequence of God's judgments (Rev 8:6-12; 16:3-4, 8, 17-20). Of course, the real cause of this destruction is sinful mankind and their satanic leadership who will, during the Day of the Lord, continue to pursue policies and practices that defile and consequently destroy the earth (Rev 11:18; Isa 24:5-6; Micah 7:13). Worldwide contamination of both soil and water resources will occur, much of the vegetation will be completely destroyed by fire, hail, searing heat, and other forces, and a gigantic earthquake will level mountains and sink islands worldwide, probably leaving in its wake millions of tons of debris covering formerly productive land. The disastrous accounts of Revelation 8-19 confirm previous forecasts by God of a day when: **"The Lord is going to lay waste the earth and devastate it; He will ruin its face and scatter its inhabitants"** (Isa 24:1)

Even prior to the Day of His Wrath, God has already "turned rivers into desert, flowing springs into thirsty ground, and fruitful land into a salt waste, because of the wickedness of those who lived there" (Psa 107:33-34). Either included in the events of the Day of the Lord, or delivered in the judgments of centuries past, are a number of judgments against specific nations and localities that will result in conspicuous permanent scars upon the landscape, according to God's pronouncements. Specific sites thus targeted include: Sodom and Gomorrah (Gen 19:24-25; Duet 29:23), Babylon (Isa 13:19-22; 14:22-23; Jer 50:13, 39-40; 51:24-26, 37, 42, 43), Edom (Isa 34:9-12; Jer 49:17-18; Joel 3:19), Hazor (portions of Arabia) (Jer 49:33), and Egypt (Joel 3:19).

I believe these permanent scars will persist in the Millennium, and that it will probably take centuries of restoration efforts for the earth to recover from the detrimental effects of the preceding seven years of judgment. According to Isaiah 24:20 the world will never again rise to its former height. Restoration and reconstruction will be limited initially by the relatively small populations of survivors, but will probably gradually increase in intensity in proportion to increases in the work force, and the needs to accommodate more and more people on the earth.

The Lord is gracious, and I'm sure will provide sovereign guidance and assistance. In past judgments of specific nations, He has healed those He struck (Isa 19:22), and "restored the fortunes" of some of the nations He had severely judged (Jer 48:47; 49:6, 39). However, I find no Scriptural accounts of the Lord using His power to perform miraculous changes in the international environment, as He will do for Israel. We do know that the natural resources of the nations will be restored significantly, for they will present offerings of their products and wealth to the Lord and His people.

In the premillennial world, Israel will certainly not escape the devastation wrought by God's wrath. In fact, she is #1 on His hit list (Jer 25:15-18). Because of her sin and obstinacy, she has suffered the brunt of God's judgments for a longer time and more repeatedly than any other nation (Isa 9:8-10:4; Joel 1:4-7), having been required to pay double for her sins (Isa 40:2). Consequently, on the eve of the Millennium, the Land of Israel will be scarred by the devastations of many generations (Isa 61:4), and will have become "a perpetual wilderness" (Ezek 38:8 MLB). Then, as already described in the outline, the Spirit of God will transform both the people and their land, creating the world's greatest wonder, and the marvel and joy of all the earth. The transforming work of God will result in a quality of people and environment that will be distinctly superior to all other nations. Thus the Lord will fulfill His promise that His people "will inherit a double portion in their land" (Isa 61:7), and Israel will be recognized by the nations as those whom the Lord has blessed (Isa 61:9). The Lord will use this disparity, not to belittle or discourage the nations, but to display His own attributes, and help draw men from every nation to the knowledge of Himself. However, Satan will eventually call men's attention to Israel's prosperity for an entirely different purpose! When he is

The Millennial Kingdom

released from imprisonment in the Abyss, at the termination of the 1,000 years, he will deceive the nations and provoke an attack on Israel. A primary motivation for this attack will be a covetousness of Israel's wealth (Ezek 38:11-13).

(6) The Bible declares that the sovereign Lord "will rule with a rod (or scepter) of iron." What does this statement mean? Will He rule in such a manner as to beat His subjects into submission?

This particular description of His reign is repeated four times in the Bible. It first occurs in Psalm 2 in an angry rebuke by God to the nations and their leaders who challenge God's right to rule over them; uniting to openly rebel against Him (vs. 1-3). In answer to their mutiny, God terrifies them by announcing that He has granted His Son the authority to rule over them, and to eventually administer appropriate compensatory punishment for their rebellion. In this psalm, Christ reveals the Father's decree to Himself: "He said to Me, '…Ask of Me, and I will make the nations your inheritance, the ends of the earth your possession. You will rule them (other possible translations: "break them," or "shepherd them") with a rod (scepter) of iron, and you will dash them in pieces like pottery'" (vs. 7-9).

It is important to note that God follows His warning of impending judgment with some advice that offers an alternative to the rebellious leaders of the nations: "Therefore, you Kings, be wise; be warned you rulers of the earth. Serve the Lord with fear and rejoice with trembling. Kiss the Son (give Him sincere homage) lest He be angry and you be destroyed in your way, for His wrath can flare up in a moment. Blessed are all who take refuge in Him" (vs. 10-12). If the rulers will acknowledge Him as their Lord, He offers to be their refuge instead of their destroyer. This psalm discloses that God will not only display His wrath through His Son, the King, but His grace as well. It is in keeping with His righteousness to vent His anger against the sinful defiance of men, but it is also His option to forgive sin when men repent.

Another passage that confirms the fact that Christ will rule all nations with an iron scepter is **Rev 12:5**. When will He assume such authority? The context of this verse helps us answer this question. In Rev 11:15, the seventh trumpet is sounded. At that time, a loud proclamation is broadcast in heaven announcing: "The Kingdom of the world has become the Kingdom of our Lord and of His Christ, and He will reign forever and ever." In the following passage the Lord is thanked for taking His great power and beginning to reign. Several significant consequences of His assumption of sovereign power are then given. Among them is the fact that the time has arrived "to destroy those who destroy the earth" (Rev 11:18). Christ actually assumes His authority prior to the last half of the Day of the Lord.

The actual exercise of Christ's sovereign authority begins in heaven with the defeat of Satan and His angels, and their subsequent casting down to earth; the eternal exile from heaven of the one who used it as a base of operations for fulfilling his purposes as "the god of this world" (a role temporarily allowed by God). When this cleansing is completed, a second loud proclamation is made: "**Now** have come the salvation and the power and the Kingdom of our God, and **the authority of His Christ**" (Rev 12:10). This evidently includes His authority identified in verse 5, "to rule with a scepter of iron."

Even before being seated on His throne in Jerusalem, while the Day of His wrath still runs its course, Christ will hold the iron scepter in His grasp, ready to dash in pieces the rebellious leaders of earth and their followers. The destruction of Mystery Babylon will be an example of His wrath in action, as will the various vial judgments. Then at the end of the Day of the Lord, the King of kings and Lord of lords appears on a white horse, leading the armies of heaven in a charge to earth to exterminate the Beast and his armies. This is the final time that Psa 2:9 is quoted: "Out of His mouth comes a sharp sword with which to strike down the nations. '**He will rule them with an iron scepter.**' He treads the winepress of the fury of the wrath of God Almighty (Rev 19:15). Note that His dreadful judgment is directed against those who persistently resist Him and challenge His authority; those who have assembled at Armageddon to unitedly and openly oppose Him. The subsequent annihilation of His enemies actually occurs just prior to the beginning of His thousand year reign on earth. This event, the War of the Sovereign God's Great Day, and the destruction of earth's rebellious people 1,000 years later, following Satan's release from the Abyss, probably represent the two principle times when God's Son will carry out that portion of the Father's decree recorded in Psa 2:9. In both events He will be judging unrepentant rebels.

I conclude that the Son's rule with a scepter of iron describes the firmness (resolve) and severity with which He will judge human mutiny, but does not picture the manner in which He will conduct the daily affairs of His Kingdom. In the 1,000 year administration of His royal office on the current earth, the King will display all of His attributes (as already pointed out in part A of the outline of Period III). From His throne decrees will go forth upholding truth and righteousness, but grace and lovingkindness will be extended to His citizens as well. "In lovingkindness a throne will be established; in faithfulness a Man will sit on it, …One who in judging seeks justice and speeds the cause of righteousness" (Isa 16:5). His throne room will be a place where "lovingkindness and truth meet together, righteousness and peace kiss each other" (Psa 85:10).

This is not to say that Christ will not be firm in His demands for obedience to His will. The nations will recognize that there will be serious consequences for noncompliance. For example, the survivors of the nations that formerly attacked Israel (probably referencing the time of the Jews great misery), will be required to come to Jerusalem each year at the Feast of the Tabernacles to worship the King (Zech 14:16). "If any of the peoples of earth do not go up to Jerusalem to worship the King, the Lord Almighty, they will have no rain" (Zech 14:17). Another responsibility given the nations is to show respect to Israel by offering them service. The consequences of refusing or neglecting to provide such respect is clearly spelled out: "For the nation or kingdom that will not serve you (Israel) will perish; it will be utterly ruined" (Isa 60:12).

These are tough words, but they are not malicious! They represent the standards of a righteous and benevolent Lord, and not the demands of an unfeeling and heavy handed taskmaster. Psalm 72 speaks of the era when "He will rule from sea to sea, and from the River to the ends of the earth" (vs. 8). During this time it is said: "All kings will bow down to Him and all nations will serve Him (vs. 11). But the psalm also discloses why they will serve Him: "**For He will deliver the needy who cry out, and the afflicted who have no one to help. He will take pity on the weak and needy and save the needy from death. He will rescue them from oppression and violence for precious is their blood in His sight**" (vs. 12-14). A little later the psalm discloses that: "**All** nations will be blessed through Him, and all nations will call Him blessed" (vs. 17).

(7) What form of worship will be practiced in Israel?

In the section of the outline describing Jerusalem, I barely mentioned the functions of the priests and Levites, and included nothing concerning the kind of formal worship which the priests will administer, and the Levites help facilitate by performing supporting tasks. Though the subject of this future worship is not detailed in its entirety in the Bible, enough is included in Ezekiel's description of the Millennial Temple, and of the functions of the priesthood and "the Prince" (A leader in Israel distinct from the Lord), to allow us to formulate a picture of certain aspects of public worship.

The Lord, of course, will be the focal point of worship, and His Temple on Mt. Zion will be designed to accommodate the various elements and participants of the prescribed worship (Ezek 40:38-46; 41:21-22; 42:13-14; 43:10-17; 46:19-24). Very little information is provided us concerning the ministry of the priests directly to the Lord within the Sanctuary of the Temple, but we are informed of the kind of services performed by the priests, on behalf of the people, within the Inner Court. These services will consist primarily of the rendering of sacrifices; **a form of worship similar in a number of respects to the sacrificial system instituted under the Old Testament and administered by the Levitical Priesthood.**

Millennial worship will include various sacrificial offerings of animals to the Lord, including dedicatory burnt offerings, peace offerings, sin offerings, and guilt offerings. Some of these will be complemented by grain offerings, and for certain feasts there will also be drink offerings (Ezek 45:17; 40:39). The Old Testament equivalent of these types of sacrifices are described in detail in the first seven chapters of Leviticus. All of the Old Testament animal sacrifices included the shedding and sprinkling of blood on the alter, but only in the case of the sin offering was the blood taken into the meeting place to be sprinkled before the Lord in front of the veil of the Most Holy Place. In the millennial worship, there will be occasions when blood will be carried into the Lord's sanctuary by ministering priests, to be presented to the Lord at His table (altar) (Ezek 44:15).

A select and holy priesthood (the descendents of Zadok) will have the exclusive responsibility for final preparation and offering of sacrifices, which duties will be carried out within the inner court where the alter resides. This priesthood will also minister to the Lord within His Sanctuary (Ezek 44:15-16).

The Levites will serve as custodians and guards of the Temple and assist the people in worship by receiving and slaughtering their burnt offerings. Their work stations and duties will be confined to the outer court of the temple, which is also accessible to the people at appropriate times.

The Prince will serve as custodian of the peoples required contributions of livestock, grain and oil, to be used as offering on Sabbaths, New Moons, and designated feasts (festivals). He will appear just inside the eastern gate of the inner court of the temple to provide these offerings, on behalf of the people, at the appropriate times.

Formal worship will be initiated after the Lord, in all his glory, enters the Temple (Ezek 43:1-5), and following the erection of the Altar. The initial service will consist of a seven day period in which a series of sacrifices are made to sanctify the altar (Set it apart to the Lord through cleansing and purification) (Ezek 43:18-26). Following this cleansing of the altar, from the eighth day onward, the priests will utilize the altar to present offerings on behalf of the people.

There will be continual daily burnt offerings to the Lord of a lamb and cereal offerings, morning by morning (Ezek 46:13-15). On the Sabbath there shall be burnt offerings and peace offerings. The burnt offerings on the Sabbath shall consist of six lambs and one ram, all without blemish. This same sacrifice will be made at the new moon but with the addition of a bullock without blemish. Twice a year there shall be special blood offerings of a bullock; on new year's day to purify the Sanctuary (Ezek 45:19), and on the first day of the second half of the year to make atonement for anyone who has sinned through error or ignorance (Ezek 45:20).

Sacrifices are also prescribed for specified feasts. In the Spring, at the combined Passover/Feast of Unleavened Bread, a sin offering will be made on Passover for all the people of the land, followed by burnt offerings and sin offerings on all seven of the following days of the feast (Ezek 45:21-24). The same provisions for sin offerings and burnt offerings will be made at the Autumn Feast of Ingathering (Feast of Tabernacles or Booths) (Ezek 45:25).

Does the sacrificial system to be instituted in Israel during the Millennium seem foreign to New Covenant realities? I must admit it does to me, and I am sure other Christians have questioned the need for continuing animal sacrifices following Christ's offering Himself for sin on our behalf; an offering of one sacrifice for sins forever (Heb 10:12). "**For by one offering He has perfected for all time those who are thus consecrated**" (Heb 10:14 NEB).

The various Old Covenant sacrifices prescribed by God, temporarily attained atonement, forgiveness of unknown and known sin, removal of guilt, and restoration of peace. In addition they were designed to please the Lord. The New Covenant, made possible by the death and resurrection of Christ, accomplished all these blessings and objectives conclusively and permanently: "'**This is the covenant I will make with them after those days', says the Lord: 'I will set My laws in their hearts and write them on their understanding;' then He adds, 'and their sins and wicked deeds I will remember no more at all.' And where these have been forgiven, there is no longer any offering for sins**" (Heb 10:16-18 NEB).

This new covenant was made with the houses of Israel and Judah (Jer 31:31-34; Heb 8:8-12) and it is my understanding, supported by various Scriptural passages already noted in the outline, that all Israel, during Christ's millennial reign, will be participants in the New Covenant; forgiven of sin and filled with His Spirit. When the Letter to the Hebrews was written, the First (Old) Covenant was already said to be antiquated and obsolete, and to be approaching the vanishing point (shortly disappear) (Heb 8:13). **Why then are sacrifices which were rendered obsolete seemingly reinstituted**? A number of Christian scholars have wrestled with similar questions, and come to the conclusion that the primary function of such Millennial sacrifices is to mirror what Christ already accomplished on behalf of the participants in such worship; to portray and reinforce in the minds of worshipers His offering of Himself for them.

Bible commentators use variable terms to describe the Millennial sacrifices, such as "memorials", "object lessons", "symbols", etc., but generally agree that such future animal sacrifices are not the means of obtaining cleansing from sin. Rather they will serve as reminders of the single sacrifice by the Lamb of God that makes eternal forgiveness possible. It has been proposed that Millennial offerings will point back to Christ's death in a similar manner as old testament sacrifices pointed ahead; both focusing on Christ's completely effective sacrifice, once for all.

God, without doubt, does have legitimate and righteous reasons for putting in place, in His future earthly Kingdom, the form of worship described to us by Ezekiel, and alluded to elsewhere in the Scriptures as well (ex. Jer 33:18). The foregoing statements concerning the memorial value of the offerings may very well describe the primary reason for reinstituting animal sacrifices during the Millennium. However, **I would like the readers to consider a possible additional reason.**

The Millennial Kingdom

On page 111 of the outline, under the topic, "Fruition in the Land," a couple of objectives of God for the Kingdom were proposed. One of these purposes of God for this future period was to use Israel to sanctify Himself in the eyes and minds of the nations (Ezek 39:27); **to use the very nation who's attitudes and actions brought Him disgrace and disrespect, to set the record straight by projecting a true image of His glory**.

The world's perspective of the Lord's holiness and purposes will dramatically improve during the Millennial Kingdom, as the nations witness His will and ways being exhibited through His people, and the resulting blessings. To display such righteousness through Israel, God may choose to "rerun" some of their history, using a familiar setting but a completely revised script; to take Israel back in time to the point where they deviated from His purposes for them and give them a second chance, so to speak; **to empower Israel to actually display the kind of life that should have been originally lived under the Theocratic system of government and Levitical form of worship that He had originally established for them**. However, this time around, He will empower them, through His Spirit and personal leadership, to accomplish His purposes. They will no longer rely on their own ability to keep His law. God's sovereign intervention, empowerment, and blessings will be evident to the nations, and the defaced image of the Creator, that Israel had formerly projected, will be erased.

The nations had never understood the holiness of God because Israel had been insensitive to His holiness. They built residences and tombs for their kings in very close proximity to the Lord's Temple (Ezek 43:7-9). They also admitted foreigners and strangers of God's covenant into His house (temple); even hiring the ungodly to assist in presenting offerings in the stead of the priests (Ezek 44:7-8). In all aspects of millennial worship God's holiness will be given special consideration, including the design of the temple (Ezek 43:10-11), the zoning of the temple mount (Ezek 43:12); admittance to the temple (Ezek 44:9); the selection, dress code, and rules of conduct of the priesthood (Ezek 44:15-22); and the teaching presented to the general public (Ezek 14:23). Consequently, "**They will keep My Name Holy, they will acknowledge the holiness of the Holy One of Israel**" (Isa 29:23).

Correct worship will be an essential part of Israel's responsibility to convey a true concept of God to the nations. **The international community never understood the purpose or value of Israel's religion, because they formerly witnessed only a perverted substitute for true worship of the Lord**. Leading such misrepresentation had been the very men selected by God to provide spiritual leadership. "'Both prophet and priest are godless, even in My temple I find their wickedness,' declares the Lord" (Jer 23:11). Some of the Levites had actually assisted and led the people in worship of idols (Ezek 44:12). In the Millennial Temple, the priests who serve the Lord will be completely separated to Him; even to the extent that he becomes their only inheritance and possession (Ezek 44:28). Their holiness and maturity will qualify them to teach the people to be spiritually discerning, to serve as judges in the settlement of any disputes among the people, and to lead in the worship of the Lord on all Sabbaths and Festivals, assuring that all the Lord's rules and regulations are observed; maintaining the sacredness of these times (Ezek 44:23-24).

God's people had corrupted their prescribed worship of the Lord in a number of ways. To begin with, their hearts (motives, attitudes) were wrong: "These people come near to Me with their mouth, but their hearts are far from me, their worship of Me is made up only of rules taught by men" (Isa 29:13). Some of God's people had actually concluded that it was vain and unnecessary to worship the Lord (Mal 3:13-15).

In the Millennial Kingdom, sincerity will return to worship, as men and women truly revere God. Such reverence will be reflected in their thoughts, conversations, and actions. **This change of heart will be obvious to the nations who will "once more (be able to) distinguish between the righteous and the wicked, between one who serves God and one who does not serve Him"** (Mal 3:16-18 MLB). This transformation, of course, will be the result of God's heart transplant; "I will give them a heart to know Me, that I am the Lord. They will be My people, and I will be their God, for they will return to Me with all their hearts" (Jer 24:7).

Historically, not only had Israel's worship been insincere, but it was conducted in a corrupt manner. They cheated God with their sacrifices and offerings, polluting His alter with animals that were blemished (blind, lame, sick, killed by predators, etc.) (Mal 1:7-9, 12-14). While the heathen held God in awe, His people defaced His image by their disrespect (vs. 14). They also robbed God of His rightful tithe (Mal 3:8-9).

During the Millennium, regeneration of God's people will result in restoration of sincerity and truth to their worship of the Lord: "For on My Holy Mountain, the mountain height of Israel, says the Lord God, all the house of Israel, **all of them, shall serve Me** in the land: there I will accept them, and there **I will require your contributions and the choicest of your gifts**, with all your sacred offerings. **As a pleasant fragrance will I accept you…and through you I will be sanctified in the sight of the nations.**" (Ezek 20:40-41 MLB).

When the people of Israel faithfully make their annual proportional contributions of animals and grain to the Lord, and daily offerings of **unblemished** animals are sacrificed to Him, the world will observe. When tithing is again practiced, and God consequently abundantly blesses the givers, the nations will take notice (Mal 3:10-12). **Worldwide respect for God will be regained, and His prophetic declaration will be fulfilled: "For from the rising of the sun to its setting, My name shall be great among the nations, and in every place incense shall be offered to My Name, a pure offering; for My name shall be great among the nations, says the Lord of hosts"** (Mal 1:11 MLB).

Though most of the worship taking place at the Temple in Jerusalem will be limited to the Jewish nation, representatives of the nations who attacked Israel, during her hour of great misery, will come up annually to celebrate the Feast of Booths (Zech 14:16-19). Also "the foreigners who join themselves to the Lord, to minister to Him and to love the Name of the Lord, and to be His servants;" these will be invited into full fellowship with His people and enjoy all the privileges and benefits of worship and prayer in His House (Isa 56: 6-8 MLB).

Period Four: The Final Conflict

IV. Period Four: The Final Conflict

Introduction

World War I, which concluded in 1918, was labeled by the media of that day as "**The War To End All Wars.**" Many of those who signed the Armistice agreement in Geneva, Switzerland, at the termination of that great international confrontation shared that optimism. To help assure world-wide peace, they established the League of Nations.

Scarcely twenty years later came a second war of global proportions, considerably larger than its predecessor and much more deadly. Following its cessation, men again sought to maintain world peace by establishing an organization devoted to promoting mutual understanding in the international community. By making this organization more cosmopolitan, more powerful, more permanent, and more involved in current international concerns and needs, some of the world's leaders hoped to permanently resolve the ethnic, religious, political and economic differences existing between and within member nations.

Since the establishment of the United Nations in October 1945, wars and rumors of wars have steadily increased, fueled by man's passions and his production of weapons, both of which are escalating out of control. While men still speak of resolving conflicts through negotiations, treaties, cooperative ventures, etc., they have pretty much resigned themselves to accepting, or at least tolerating war. Frequently the United Nations attempts only to control the level to which conflicts escalate, and even in this endeavor, their feeble and misguided efforts fail miserably. The problem can never be solved by those that represent half of the problem.

Despite man's failure to either curtail or control war, and the prevailing pessimism that war will ever be abolished, **there actually will be a war to end all wars.** This end-time confrontation will probably be of greater magnitude than any of its predecessors, but it will have the same casual agents as all of them, i.e., it will be instigated by Satan and promoted by the lusts of men. Unregenerate mankind is highly qualified for starting wars (Jas 4:1-3), but doesn't have a clue as to what it takes to bring about their cessation. In the case of the final conflict, that will be no problem because God, not man, will be the terminator. It is the Lord who will stop it abruptly and establish a permanent peace, terminating both war and its causes forever. He will produce an everlasting armistice written in the hearts of men and not on paper.

Shortly after the Sovereign Lord brings this war to a close, He will also terminate all clocks, calendars, time zones, and work shifts. There will be no more day time, night time, standard time, daylight saving time, prime time, on time, over time, short time, long time, fast time, slow time, spring time, summer, fall, or winter time. The sun, moon, and stars will all start drawing unemployment. The war to end all wars will mark the transition from time to eternity. The survivors of the final war, following God's formal judging of the lost, will take up residence in a new heaven and a new earth (Rev 21:1-5). World history, as we know it, will have taken its last step, and the remnant citizens of God's Kingdom will begin their refreshing and peaceful march through eternity. Absolute perfection will be realized as all things in heaven and on earth are brought together in Christ. This is the itinerary predetermined by God before time even began (Eph 1:4-10).

A. The Mystery War

The final confrontation of all time is given no name in the bible, but it seems quite fitting that its title should remain questionable for I find its very occurrence somewhat of a mystery. Why did God, in eternity past, choose to draw the curtain of human history closed with a war? Why won't time run out on the present earth as it began, with God's creation enjoying peace, prosperity, and a righteous relationship with their Creator?

As we have discovered, numerous wars and rumors of wars are scheduled to take place throughout the first two end time periods covered in our study. The devastation caused by these conflicts will reach unimaginable proportions during the Day of the Lord when attacks by demonic forces will be followed by destructive conquests by the ten armies of the Beast. Framing this seven year period, and sandwiched in its middle, will occur three conflicts of particular consequence to God's people: (1) the Great Tribulation to be experienced by the Jews, (2) the midweek attack of the Beast upon the Jewish remnant, and (3) The War of the Sovereign God's Great Day, in which the Church participates. Within these seven plus years, associated with the opening of the fifth, sixth, and seventh seals by Christ, will occur the greatest concentration of conflicts in earth's history, and the greatest suffering and death experienced by its residents since the great flood. Within just a few years, God "will make man scarcer than pure gold" (Isa 13:12).

By contrast, the last great world-wide confrontation will be separated from the period of concentrated destruction by centuries of peace, reconstruction, international cooperation, environmental blessing, and best of all, righteous rule under the very Creator of the universe. Depending on the life span of the unredeemed segment of mankind living on earth during the Millennium, it is possible that numerous generations of that era will cycle through world history without ever once experiencing wars of even hearing rumors of such. In fact their world will be one devoid of both weapons and armies (Isa 2:4). As far as these future intermediate Kingdom generations are concerned, the Lord's victory achieved at Armageddon will have constituted the war that ended all wars. And well it might, except that God has prearranged a different agenda, one that includes a final conflict of perhaps even greater magnitude than that War of the Sovereign Lord's Great Day. Strange as it may seem, at the very end of time, the most imposing human army ever assembled will literally cover the land as a mighty cloud, advancing on Israel with the intentions of looting its rich treasures, destroying its righteous people, and even conquering its eternal King (Rev 20:7-9).

All the end-time wars which will precede the Millennium are quite predictable. Given the facts concerning the spiritual, moral, and political climate of those times, it is easy to understand how wars would naturally precipitate. For example, it is not difficult to conceive how an attack could be launched upon Israel by an international force in the near future. World-wide, we currently see enmity in men's hearts toward the Jews. We are already living in days when people are "lovers of themselves, avaricious, boasters, haughty, abusive, disobedient to parents, ungrateful, irreverant, without natural affection, relentless, slanderous, uncontrolled, brutal, with no love for good, treacherous, rash, conceited, lovers of pleasure rather than lovers of God" (II Tim 3:2-4 MLB). It is relatively easy to visualize how current problems, divisions, hatred, and terrorism in the Middle East could erupt into "Israel's time of great distress."

The Final Conflict

Likewise, during the Day of the Lord, that will shortly follow that abbreviated time of misery, all the factors contributing to conflict will be stacked in favor of war. Earth's Gentile residents entering the Day of the Lord, i.e., those without God's seal, will have individually and collectively rejected God's message of salvation and His attempts to bring them to repentance. As a result, their hearts will be completely hardened, and they will be united in total rebellion against their creator (Rev 9:20-32; 11:9, 10, 18). As if this were not enough, Satan, who is a master of deception with a history of leading individuals and nations astray, will personally be present on the earth with his demons, exercising all his deceptive power through the Beast (Rev 12:9; 13:2-4; 16:13, 14). Given such a climate of rebellion (Dan 8:12), and such a cast of supernatural enemies of God, peace is an impossibility. Thus, though we may not be able to visualize the devastation that will occur, we can readily understand the fact that major conflicts will characterize that chaotic period of future history known as "the Day of the Lord."

By contrast, it is difficult to understand how the final war will ever become a reality, though by faith we accept the fact that it will. We have only limited information given us in the Bible concerning this conflict, but lack of information is not what makes its reality difficult to comprehend. Rather, from a human point of view, it is difficult to come up with a logical explanation of why it should happen. Why should the people of the world want deliverance from a reign of peace; from circumstances that have been overwhelmingly and consistently positive? Why would they want to overthrow a King that has administered perfect justice and treated them with respect; one who has made major contributions to their personal and international well being? As we have already noted in this study, all the nations existing on the earth during the Millennium will be cognizant of Christ's glory and recognize that His righteousness has brought stability, peace, and prosperity to the earth. Why would they ever want to overthrow a government of proven integrity and success? In the final segment of this commentary on post millennial events, we will attempt to answer this question. At that point we will note the exceeding deception of sin, and how totally impoverished an unregenerate mind can be. You probably already recognize this void in mankind's spiritual dimension and thus this prophetic war does not seem as improbable as I may have pictured it to be.

B. The Scene and the Enactment of the Mysterious Revolt

What would you do if you awoke one morning and observed the scene described in the following sentence from your favorite viewpoint, the large gold trimmed bay windows facing the beautiful northern mountains? As far as your eye could see, though partially obscured by a giant dust cloud, were fierce and well armed warriors mounted on prancing horses and advancing in your direction. What would you do? How would you react? Would you rush out to first shut your gate? What if you had no gate? What if none of the houses had fences, walls, or gates? Would you call 911 for the police or the National Guard? What if no protective agencies or armies were in existence in your entire land, and no citizen owned any kind of defensive weapon? Would you follow the standard steps outlined in the phone book for handling this type of emergency? What if you, and your ancestors before you, had enjoyed unbroken peace and quietness in the same location for 1,000 years; experiencing not a single unpleasant interruption or any kind of trouble?

I'm sure we have some difficulty visualizing such a peaceful and safe haven, but I'm equally sure that if we actually did enjoy such safety, and then were suddenly subjected to such an attack, we would feel disoriented, helpless, and terrified. It is theoretically possible that someone could experience this very kind of perplexing and fearful encounter if they happened to be living in northern or central Israel in the year 1001 ACR (After Christ's Return). At that time, right on prophetic schedule, the largest cavalry/infantry combination ever assembled will advance on Israel from the north. Their shields glinting in the shafts of sunlight penetrating the dust, they will cover the entire landscape to the very limits of the distant horizons. "Advancing like a storm–like a cloud covering the land" (Ezek 38:9). "In number they are like the sand of the seashore" (Rev 20:8).

Though the attack upon Israel from the north, following the Millennium, will certainly take place, the fearful experience alluded to will probably not be experienced by a single Jewish resident living in the land at that time. No citizen of the Lord's holy nation will be at home when the enemy attacks. They won't even be in their tribal province, but rather encamped around their King in Jerusalem; along with all their families, relatives, friends, and fellow citizens (Rev 20:9). Forewarned by the omniscient Christ of the impending attack, they will have evacuated their unprotected villages and, unhurriedly, moved through the most beautiful landscape on earth to facilities prepared for them in the Capitol.

I speculate such a scenario based on God's promises to Israel for those days. Centuries before they even began their 1,000-year sojourn in the earthly Kingdom ruled over by Christ, the remnant of Israel were promised that their reestablishment would be protected by the Lord–they would never again be humiliated or plundered by foreigners (Isa 54:4, 14, 17; Jer 32:37; Ezek 34:28). Thus I am confidant that none of God's people will experience the wrath of the invading host. The Bible lists absolutely no casualties among the "quiet people who dwell securely without walls to defend them without bars and without gates" (Ezek 38:11 MLB).

Let's now return for another look at the attacking host. Who are they and where did they come from? To answer this question we will consider all three dimensions of the host spread out on the mountains of Israel; their breadth or geographic origin, their depth or political affiliation, and their height or spiritual motivation.

The host will be very wide, i.e., it will include soldiers from ancestries, regions, and nations both large and small. Ezekiel provides us with the specific names of some of the nations and regions providing troops. It's a real challenge for present-day Bible scholars to correlate all the ancient names referenced by the Prophet with nations and regions which will exist in the still distant future, but it seems likely that armies from regions we now know as Iran, Iraq, Sudan, Ethiopia, Libya and Turkey will be included. Also armies from other nations along the northern coastline of the Mediterranean Sea, "troops from the far north" (possible reference to portions of the former USSR), and "many others" (Ezek 38:3-6). Thus we know that at least the continents of Asia, Europe, and Africa will be represented in the powerful international alliance that will attack Israel.

If you and I were writing a script for a present-day confrontation between Israel and her enemies, we might choose to also include Jordon, Egypt, and certainly Syria, in the ranks of the invading host. To be sure, these nations, as well as other immediate neighbors of Israel, have traditionally hated the Jews and sought to destroy their nation. However, environmental, political, and spiritual changes are scheduled to take place during the Millennium that will profoundly alter both the geography of these lands and the character of their people.

For example, the borders of Israel itself will be extended to include portions of the land now administered by some of these unfriendly neighbors (Ezek 47:13-20). Another portion will become an uninhabitable buffer zone. In particular, a segment of Jordon, previously recognized as ancient Edom, will be blitzed by judgments that reduce its environment to a desolate owl habitat; becoming a unique but uninviting wildlife sanctuary (Isa 34:8-17).

Even more significant are the changes God will bring about in some specific neighbors' hearts to remove their animosity toward the Jews. Can you picture a three nation alliance composed of Israel, Egypt, and Syria? What about a holy alliance of these three nations in which they covenant together to love and serve the living God? That's exactly what the Lord will bring about during the Millennium. He will not just bring them to a peace table, but will make them brothers and unite their nations in a holy triad (Isa 19:23-25). The citizenry of certain Gentile trading centers that will exist on Israel's western and south eastern borders will also be excluded from the army that comes against Israel. In fact, when these people observe the invasion, they will question the evil motives of the aggressors (Ezek 38:13).

The Final Conflict

Now let's consider the second dimension of the invading armies, i.e., their political affiliation. It is apparent from the Biblical record that when this vast host moves into Israel they are well organized and well armed (Ezek 38:4). This apparent preparedness for battle is another mystery of this war. At the beginning of the Millennium the entire world will be disarmed, their weapons converted to agricultural implements, their armies disbanded, and their military academies closed. For 1,000 years no nation will engage in any type of warfare (Isa 2:4). That being the case, where will this future army get their weapons and how will they learn to operate as a well oiled and coordinated fighting machine? We would logically assume that to ready a force of such diversity and magnitude would require time for considerable planning and preparation. This assumption is confirmed by the Bible record.

"Many days" prior to their "D day" appointment, a prominent international leader will begin to organize and prepare the nations for their historical confrontation with God (Ezek 38:7-8). But such advance action, though it may explain the battle readiness of the troops, introduces a further element of mystery into this future war. How in the world could the nations possibly get away with such a gigantic demonstration of planning, production, and training without Christ, who it is said "will rule with a rod of iron," getting wind of it, and consequently, bringing their actions to a screeching halt?

The answer to the first half of the proceeding question is that their treacherous actions will not go undetected by the Lord. He predicted this mutiny (Joel 3:9-12). However, though He is cognizant of the entire scenario, He will not intervene to stop it. In fact, He will not only allow them to proceed but will offer undetected encouragement to their effort. He will actually control their decisions and movements, dragging them toward the supposed fulfillment of their own evil goals–their appointment with destruction (Ezek 38:4).

The Lord will choose a human leader whom He particularly opposes, to organize the end-time alliance of nations, provide it with political and military leadership, and eventually bring it into Satan's camp. The individual chosen for this task is none other that "Gog" (Ezek 38:3-4). You will recall that this was also the name of a prominent military leader in the Battle of the Sovereign Lord's Great Day (Ezek 39:1, 2). When we studied that battle, destined to take place at Armageddon, we suggested that there is a possibility that the name Gog might even be used as a synonym for Satan, who will participate in both of the last two great conflicts. However, the name "Gog" is probably more likely used to identify human leaders, i.e., two separate key field generals associated with each of the last two great wars; a symbolic title used to identify an individual in each conflict who will more or less play the same role, that of being Satan's chief puppet. In both wars, Gog is identified as the leader of nations deluded and mustered to war by the Devil, but actually controlled and manipulated by God. In both wars, Gog is an individual who will initiate and promote the hatred of Satan, but fulfill the plan of God.

In the battle of Armageddon, the name Gog may be synonymous with the Beast, also referred to as AntiChrist. Following that brief but devastating conflict, the Beast will be thrown into the everlasting Lake of Fire. Since his earthly termination will come a full 1,000 years prior to Conflict #4, he will no longer be a valid candidate for the title "Gog" at the time of the final war. In fact, his entire force will lie buried in the Valley of Gog's Horde.

The Gog who will command the army in the final conflict would have been well advised to visit that graveyard and view the vacant city of the dead located there, the City called "Horde" (Ezek 39:11, 16). That spacious but deathly quiet metropolis will serve as a 100-decade reminder of the utter folly of bringing a force against Christ, no matter what its size. Evidently Gog #2 will reject the loathsome message which will resound from that graveyard (Ezek 39:21; Isa 66:23-24), for he is destined to blindly lead the armies of earth in an equally futile attack on Christ, carrying them to a terrible and an eternal destruction. This madman will probably be on the scene prior to the time of Satan's release from the Abyss, leading a political organization held in readiness for the Devil to completely deceive and utilize to do his bidding.

That takes us to the third dimension of the attacking force, i.e., its spiritual motivation. It is Satan himself who leads the nations astray and assures their final doom. However, we will reserve further discussion of his role, and the lies he utilizes to motivate his troops, until the final segment of our study. Let's now turn our focus from the composition of the attacking force to its actions, as we observe the progress of the battle and it consequences.

We already mentioned that the vast host will cross Israel's border from the north. Because they meet no opposition, and likely find only villages already emptied of most of the wealth accumulated over the preceding 1,000 years, the armies will probably proceed south quite rapidly. Thus they should arrive within sight of their ultimate objective, Jerusalem, within a few days. Remember, they will be on horseback or afoot, and not riding in swift armored cars or tanks.

They shouldn't have much trouble finding the Capital of the world, because it will quite likely be accessible from all directions via broad highways. One need only continue an ascent of Israel's mountains to reach their most prominent peak, Mt. Zion. For the entire duration of the Millennium, this mount and the city that adorns its flanks will be uplifted above all the surrounding terrain, possibly the highest point on earth at that time, and definitely the most beautiful (Isa 54:11-12). The City, that the Lord in judgment once completely "plowed like a field" (Jer 26:18; 44:2), will in that day be majestically elevated, renown for its unsurpassed beauty, treasured by the nations, "the joy of the whole earth" (Psa 48:2). What a sight will greet the covetous eyes of the troops as they move to surround the City!

To provide us with some insight into what the enemies of the Lord will see from their positions on the perimeter of Jerusalem (Rev 20:9), let's pause briefly to survey for ourselves the City as it will appear on that future day.

Crowning the very summit of Mt. Zion will be the temple where the Lord Himself will reside; a glorious gem set upon the very pinnacle of the Mount which He will fill with His glory (Ezek 43:5-7). For 1,000 years, prior to this attack, many peoples of the world will have traveled to Jerusalem, "to the House of the God of Jacob." Motivated not by an infatuation with this most prominent of landmarks, but by a desire to walk in the paths of its Chief Occupant, eager to listen as he taught them His ways (Isa 2:3; Zech 8:22). What a contrast to the unholy horde, who on that appointed day, will make their ascent to "the Holy mountain" to seek earthly treasure in "the City of Truth" (Zech 8:3); to declare their independence from His way. In direct opposition to the Law Giver, the lawless will surround the Royal City and Temple from which His righteous laws have been heralded to the ends of the earth (Isa 2:3).

From our vantage point outside the City we note a small crystal clear stream of water flowing out of the Lord's House, from under a southerly threshold on the eastern side. This stream divides; one half of it flowing east and the other half west. As these branches cascade toward their ultimate destination in the Seas (Dead [then living] and Mediterranean), the streams continually increase in volume and intensity of flow, becoming major rivers even prior to reaching the city limits. Their waters team with an immense variety of fish and their shores are populated with evergreen and ever bearing fruits of diverse kinds and delicious flavors.

The view of such natural beauty captivates our thoughts and we temporarily forget that we are actually on a future battle field. Since the principle purpose of our visit is to discover what the attacking army will see, let's investigate the City's exterior in some detail. In order to be more knowledgeable about its defenses we will leave our panoramic viewpoint and move up to a position from where we can begin a circuit of the wall.

Such an inspection of the City's perimeter has been suggested to us by the Sons of Korah who will serve as our guides. In Psalm 48 these men conducted a prophetic tour of the Lord's future capital, noting Jerusalem's lofty position and beauty. They also observed and described armies led by foreign kings that unite to attack the City. However, their account of this invasion barely mentions the attack before describing a massive retreat by this international force, a withdrawal characterized by terror within and panic without.

What happened to precipitate this disorganized and hasty retreat? What did the armies see that brought them such fear and trembling? The writers of Psalm 48 have invited us to investigate and discover for ourselves the answer to these questions; to solve yet another mystery of the final war. "Walk about Zion, go around her, count her towers, consider well her ramparts, view her citadels, that you may tell of them to the next generation" (vs. 12-13).

If we were actually on the site of the millennial Jerusalem, and embarked upon this suggested tour, what would we discover? Certainly our observations would be aesthetically pleasing, but I suspect we would find none of the kinds of fortifications we were asked to look for and count, not even a single tower. Did the sons of Korah intend to mislead or confuse us when they specified that we should look for defense installations that do not even exist? No, they intended to call our attention to something greater than such fortifications. The very absence of these features would require that we look elsewhere for the real source of Jerusalem's strength and peace; that we look to the Lord.

The explanation of the terror that will grip the alien armies is hidden in a person, the Lord Almighty. This fact is made abundantly clear in Psalm 48. "He has shown Himself to be her fortress" (vs. 3). "God makes her secure forever" (vs. 8). The psalmists were eyewitnesses of the action whereby the Lord confirmed the above statements concerning His own role as Jerusalem's High Tower. They testified, "As we have heard, so have we seen in the City of the Lord Almighty, in the City of our God" (vs. 8).

When we complete our circuit of the wall, we too will be convinced of Jerusalem's sole source of strength. We will not conclude our tour carrying visions of the City's impregnable physical defenses but rather, marveling in its super human Defender. We will come to the same conclusion as the writers of this 48th Psalm, as stated in the last verse: **"For this God is our God for ever and ever, He will be our guide even to the end."**

In the preceding discussion we have already let the cat out of the bag, so to speak, by revealing the next step in the war. It is a giant step backward by the troops who formerly planned on being the aggressors. "When the kings joined forces, when they advanced together, they saw her (Jerusalem) and were astounded; they fled in terror. Trembling seized them there, pain like that of a woman in labor" (Psa 48:4-6).

What will they see that will bring about such fear and confusion? We have already suggested that they will not see an impregnable defense system, but in fact they will!

What they will see on that day is exactly what God had told His people centuries in advance that they would see: "Look upon Zion, the City of our festivals (remember the abundance of blessings that will be poured upon them in the Millennium), your eyes will see **JERUSALEM**, a peaceful abode, **A TENT THAT WILL NOT BE MOVED**; its stakes will never be pulled up, nor any of its ropes broken. **THERE THE LORD WILL BE OUR ALMIGHTY ONE** (Isa 33:20-21). We might add: And He's never out to lunch!

What will the Kings and their armies see? Momentarily they will see a rich plum to be plucked, a treasure to be stolen. But then they will become uneasy. Illuminating the temple area, reflected off the City walls, and emanating from all twelve of the open city gates, from the Gate of Rueben on the north clockwise to the Gate of Naphtalli on the east (Ezek 48:30-31), will come the glory of the Lord. A glory so pure, awesome, and powerful that even "the moon will be abashed and the sun ashamed" (Isa 24:23). When the armies of earth catch a glimpse of this glory they will immediately recognize how powerless and puny they really are, and retreat in disarray. To be sure, they will see a high tower, but it will be the Lord and not a physical fortification (Prov 18:10). The city's name will be: **"The Lord is There"** (Ezek 48:35).

I would like to speculate that it is not only what they will see that will strike fear in their hearts, but what they will hear as well. Oh, I'm not yet talking about the deafening sounds produced by the weapons God will unleash upon them, but rather joyful notes of grateful song. You see, the Israelites within the City will actually believe God's promises of protection: "In righteousness you will be established, tyranny will be far from you; you will have nothing to fear. Terror will be far removed; it will not come near you.

If anyone does attack you, it will not be my doing; whoever attacks you will surrender to you" (Isa 54:14-15). Their hearts fortified by His promises, the citizens of Jerusalem will go about fulfilling their normal routine. And what will be the standard operating procedure for a Jerusalemite? "From them will come songs of thanksgiving and the sound of rejoicing" (Jer 30:19). "They will come and shout for joy on the heights of Zion" (Jer 31:12). Songs of joy falling on the ears of oppressors, who are anticipating a much different kind of response from their victims, could really shake them up.

Really shaking them up is the next strategy on God's battle plan. The Lord intends to enter this war as an active participant (Isa 31:4-5). Before the Israelites conclude their songs of joy and thanksgiving, "the Lord will roar from Zion and thunder from Jerusalem; the earth and the sky will tremble. But the Lord will be a refuge for His people, a stronghold for the people of Israel" (Joel 3:16). When the wrath of God bursts forth from Jerusalem's temple and is unleashed as a mighty storm upon the enemies of God, it will not abate or change course "until He fully accomplishes the purposes of his heart" (Jer 30:23-24).

God Himself gives us a detailed account of exactly what He will do when He stops the retreating armies in their tracks and exercises His righteous judgments. Let's consider the first weapon in His arsenal.

> **"This is what will happen in that day:** When Gog attacks the land of Israel, my hot anger will be aroused, declares the Sovereign Lord. In my zeal and fiery wrath I declare that at that time **there will be a great earthquake** in the land of Israel. The fish of the sea, the birds of the air, the beasts of the field, every creature that moves along the ground, and all the people on the face of the earth will tremble at my presence. The mountains will be overturned, the cliffs will crumble and every wall will fall to the ground."
> —Ezek 38:18-20

Off the Richter scale? I guess so! This will be one of the two most devastating earthquakes ever experienced on earth, and may even exceed the intensity of the catastrophic quake to be triggered when the seventh angel pours out his vial shortly before Armageddon (Rev 16:18-20). Will the final quake destroy much of the environmental improvements and blessings produced during the preceding 1,000 years of peace and prosperity? Indeed it will. Will the land of Israel suffer extensive damage? Yes it will. But remember the time frame for this event. God is bringing down the curtain of history on this world and is about to usher in the new heavens and a new earth, wherein dwelleth righteousness (Rev 21:1, 5; II Pet 3:13). God continues His account of His counter attack; outlining the final actions.

> "I will summon a sword against Gog on all my mountains declares the Sovereign Lord. Every man's sword will be against his brother. I will execute judgment upon him with plague and bloodshed; I will pour down torrents of rain, hailstones and burning sulfur on him and his troops and on the many nations with him".
> —Ezek 38:21-22; see also Rev 20:9

Sounds like total annihilation, doesn't it. I'm sure that's the case, but this outcome shouldn't surprise us. Though we've associated this war with several mysteries, its conclusion is certainly not one of them. If you recall, Armageddon produced similar results, though the method God chose to dispatch His enemies was different.

Who has the final word in this war? God does: **"And so I will show my greatness and my holiness, and I will make myself known in the sight of many nations. Then they will know that I am the Lord"** (Ezek 38:23). Does that statement sound familiar? It should, because that was one of the purposes of Armageddon. Over a period of 1,000 years people and nations forget, don't they? Or is it that they are deluded? This question is answered in the next segment of our study.

We will pursue the progress of the war no further for time will have literally run out. There will be no clean-up required, no debriefing, no critique. Why bother? Every survivor is headed into eternity with a perfect understanding of what transpired. However, from our perspective, there may be some value in giving additional thought to clarifying the mystery we previously introduced. With this objective we move to Part C. We have reserved the announcement of one very significant post-war development until this next segment of our study, because it is an important part of the solution of the mystery.

C. The Mystery Solved

In Part A of these comments, I suggested that the final war of the ages might be referred to as "the Mystery War," but upon further consideration I concluded that this is not a fitting title. The attack upon Jerusalem will certainly not come as a surprise, for no invasion in the entire history of this present world is predicted further in advance of its actual occurrence. Likewise, there is no mystery related to what will happen in the ensuing conflict, for God has detailed its participants and progress, as well as the punishment that will result. Even the motives of men and the purposes of God, which we may find difficult to understand and explain, are clarified when we really give some Bible directed thought to answering the questions I initially introduced into this study. Why will nations, who will reap the fruits of 1,000 years of peace, afterward rebel against their perfectly righteous and just Ruler who has been responsible for bringing them such prosperity? There is a threefold explanation for such mutiny: **Satan's presence, man's nature, and the world,** a place where the two may come to terms. These three factors together make up the equation for war; they are the trio of elements which comprise "**the Mystery of Iniquity**."

Do you recall who will be imprisoned for a thousand years during Christ's millennial kingdom? That's correct; it will be Satan. And do you recall why he will be imprisoned? **So that he might not "lead astray the nations**" (Rev 20:3 MLB). And are you aware that following the thousand years he is scheduled to be released from his prison in the Abyss? When he is thus set free for a short time, guess what he will do? That's correct; **he "leads astray the nations**" (Rev 20:7). This statement, pure and simple, is the primary reason why a conflict will occur on the eve of this present world's history. God will temporarily release Satan and thus allow him the freedom to exercise his supernatural powers of deception on the world he once ruled. When granted this liberty, the Devil will commence doing what he does best, fabricate lies and implant them in the hearts of men.

Before his 1,000-year incarceration, Satan will succeed, through his demons, in persuading the kings of the earth to assemble at Armageddon to oppose their King on His return from heaven. Upon his release from the Abyss, Satan will take up where he left off, deceiving mankind into again opposing their King, then resident in His earthly palace. And Satan won't merely brainwash a small disoriented minority, he will enlist the cooperation of the vast masses of the earth within a very short time. He will have hardly introduced himself, to a population who likely have never even heard his name, when he will succeed in bringing millions of recruits into his camp.

Impossible we say! Given the prosperous environment of the Millennium, intelligent men could not be so easily beguiled into taking such illogical and immoral action on such a universal scale, in such an abbreviated time frame. If this truly is our response, then we grossly underestimate Satan's power as well as our own weakness. Iniquity is still a mystery that needs to be unveiled.

Factor A in the iniquity equation, as previously stated, is none other than Satan. Though we have repeatedly referred to his role in end-time conflicts, let's take some time at this juncture in our study to consider who he is and why he is so successful in deceiving mankind.

Satan is very likely the most powerful and distinguished creature ever created by God, excelled in beauty and power only by his Creator (Father, Son, and Holy Spirit). He was adorned with every kind of precious stone, but even more significant was his close relationship to the very glory of God Himself. As an anointed guardian Cherub he enjoyed access to the holy mount of God where he walked among the fiery stones (Ezek 28:13-14). Though I cannot begin to imagine the grandeur of such an elite and favored position, the description suggests to me that he probably enjoyed a unique and unrivaled status in the very inner circle of God; a position reserved for very few, and possibly unique to the Guardian Cherub. Whether or not he shared such a distinct office with others, we know that at one time he was a recipient of unusual grace and privilege.

This created being, also referred to as "the Shining One" and "the Son of the Dawn" (Isa 14:12 NET), was blameless in his ways from the day he was created until wickedness was found in him, at which time he became filled with violence (Ezek 28:15-16). He came to view himself as a rival of God, and determined to elevate his own throne above that of his Creator (Isa 14:13-14). Thus was initiated the spirit of selfishness and pride that has defiled the universe to this day, and resulted in continued confrontations between the forces of good and evil.

While we are considering Satan's personality and power, it should be again pointed out that **his principle trait and tool is deceit**. He is the very opposite of truth. Every since his decision to step out of the realm of truth and forsake it, he has found it incompatible with his existence, thus there is absolutely no truth in him. His library, his staff, his bait, everything Satan is and does are based on lies. That includes the fax that he may have sent to our flesh this very morning. He is a liar and the father of the lie (Jn 8:44).

Lies in themselves might not be dangerous if men could decipher them as such, but Satan has the power to camouflage them and make them appear as truth. He cannot only make the bait he utilizes in temptations appear attractive, but he is so expert at masquerading that he can transform himself into an angel of light (II Cor 11:14). We have already seen that in the Day of the Lord he will fool the world into believing that he is deity. At the very end of the ages he will probably take on a similar disguise when, after his release from the Abyss, he leads the nations astray.

As we well know, the Deceiver was in Eden the garden of God, to inject the poison of his rebellious nature into the veins of mankind (Gen 3:1-6; Ezek 28:13) and lay the groundwork for all the conflict that has transpired since that time. However, what we may not realize, or at least frequently underestimate, is the magnitude and extent of the power over mankind he still commands. Though God, through the ages, has been whittling away on Satan (Ezek 28:16), and plans even more drastic cuts prior to his final crushing (Rev 12:10; 20:1-3), our arch enemy still retains powers that supersede anything we can imagine or hope to combat in our own strength. As "the Prince of this (present) world" (Jn 12:31; 14:30; 16:11) and "the god of the present age" (II Cor 4:4), Satan absolutely controls ungodly men throughout the world, whether or not they recognize or acknowledge their slavery (Jn 8:44; I Jn 5:19). This includes individuals (Eph 2:2) and nations (Isa 14:12). He is also responsible for keeping them under his control by blinding their minds and hearts to the glory of Christ visible through the Gospel (II Cor 4:4).

Only Christ, through the Holy Spirit of God, can release men from such blindness and bondage (Jn 8:34, 36; II Cor 3:16-18; I Jn 4:4). Those of us who are freed remain absolutely dependent on the continued work of Father, Son, and Holy Spirit to prevent the evil one from overpowering us. If it were possible, i.e., if God would allow him, he would deceive even the very elect (Matt 24:24). If God were to unconditionally release us to his control we would be physically destroyed in short order (I Cor 5:5).

God allows His children, at times, to experience the strength and wrath of this enemy of our souls. Righteous Job went through such an experience when the Lord temporarily placed him at Satan's disposal (Job 1:12; 2:6). Peter learned what it meant to be sifted as wheat by Satan when Jesus granted the enemy such permission (Luke 22:31-32). Paul recognized the disabling work of Satan's messengers on his life. His torment was likewise allowed by Christ (II Cor 12:7).

There have been times when we ourselves have been the victim Satan has led almost all the way down the pathway of a particular temptation—escaping only the last step of death (Jas 1:14-15; 4:8-10; I Jn 1:8-10). There have been times when we have experienced severe heaviness of spirit because of the multitude of temptations he has brought to bear upon us (I Pet 1:6). There have been times when we couldn't

The Final Conflict

even comprehend what was going on, so severe has been his attack (I Pet 4:12). There may be times when we despair even of life, when we pass the sentence of death on ourselves knowing full well that we don't have the strength to overcome his overwhelming opposition (II Cor 1:8-9).

Fortunately for the child of God, at such times God is for us and not against us (Rom 8:31); His grace is sufficient to strengthen us (II Cor 12:9); God's inseparable love prevents us from being condemned or conquered (Rom 8:31-39); Christ faithfully prays for our complete deliverance (Luke 22:32; Heb 7:25); the Holy Spirit living within us possesses greater power than our attacker (I Jn 4:4); we are provided from God's arsenal with weapons that can be utilized by the Holy Spirit to resist and overcome our enemy (Eph 6:10-18); we are given a battle plan that has been proven successful (Rev 12:11); and the body of Christ comes to our assistance (II Cor 1:10-11; Jas 5:14-20). If it were not for these resources in Christ we would be recaptured to do Satan's will (II Tim 2:26).

Each of us has experienced to some degree the power and wrath of Satan's attacks upon us, and likewise witnessed the counterattacks by God on our behalf. Despite the Lord's past victories, some of them tainted by our lack of trust, one of the most difficult things we are asked to do as Christians is to count the temptations of Satan a joy (Jas 1:2-3). Though his attacks will never be pleasant, special blessing is promised to those who endure such treatment (Jas 1:12).

Why are Satan's temptations so difficult to endure? How do we account for the leverage he holds over mankind? Why will the nations so readily accept Satan's leadership prior to the final war?

To answer the above questions let's now examine **the second of the triad of factors that account for the mystery of iniquity**. We need not look any further than our own body. Resident within us is a selfish nature which possesses uncontrollable appetites. "**The Flesh**" is the reason we so readily follow the path of temptation to its destructive end (Jas 1:14-15). The flesh is the reason we are so willing to enter into warfare against God and man (Jas 4:1-4). Even "moral" men cannot successfully resist the law of sin and death resident within them (Rom 7:20-23).

Satan is quite familiar with this espionage agent within us. It constitutes the key to his successful recruiting program for the final war. He knows his army will be well staffed because he possesses the power to appeal to and control the sin nature. The fact that his recruits will come out of a righteous and peaceful society is of little concern to him. The only thing that matters is that they have not been regenerated, and evidently multitudes among the nations will be in that category. Satan knows that unbelief leaves their minds and consciences open for defilement (Titus 1:15). He recognizes that the unbelieving heart is "deceitful above all things and desperately wicked" (Jer 17:9 KJV).

Most of us would readily admit that the flesh is indeed weak and represents a ready port of entry for Satan. However, we may still question the Devil's ability to collectively and swiftly deceive the nations and enlist the full support of millions of recruits. If there remain any such doubts, we need only review some Bible history.

At the beginning of time, Satan appealed to Eve's appetites, and successfully deceived her when she was living in an environment more perfect than that which will occur in the Millennium. And he didn't waste many words in leading her down temptation's path.

Righteous Noah and his sons were to begin anew after generations of Satan's work were destroyed. Prior to the flood, God said to Noah, "I see the end of all humanity, for through them the earth is filled with a lust for power" (Gen 6:13 MLB). Did the flood erase this expression of Satanic pride, or free men from his dominion over their lives? No, in a few generations men gathered on a plain in the Shinar territory (Babylon), but not to worship the Lord. Instead, they were there to follow Satan's lead and "make themselves famous" (Gen 11:4 MLB). The pride of life was once again being displayed as prominently as it was prior to the cleansing flood.

Later, God made Himself known to a select nation. He miraculously delivered Israel from Egypt, guided them, provided for them, and led them to multiple victories as they conquered the promised land. Did they steadfastly cleave to the One who lived and worked in their very midst? No, in a very short time they fell away into gross sin, and worshiped images designed by the god of this world. They were seduced despite their unique status and the miracles they had personally witnessed.

Fixing up the environment, time, good times, good government, miracles, all common to the Millennium, none of these conditions or events will change the hearts of men. If even the perfect law of God cannot alone overcome the law of sin and death resident within us (Rom 7:22-23), how can we ever expect an imperfect environment to produce such a victory. Thus Satan will not have to look very far to find multitudes willing to accept his pitch, at the end of time. His strategy is simple. He will appeal to the desires of men's flesh, the desires of their eyes, and their relish for the self life (pride).

What tool will Satan use to make his pitch to the nations effective? What will he use as bait in making his appeal to men's sinful appetites? This question brings us to **the third element of the iniquity equation, i.e., "the World."**

This term, frequently used in the New Testament, identifies psychological, biological, physical, social, and economic elements in our environment that have been perverted by Satan. He has taken the very creation which God established for our well being and transformed it into a playpen for the flesh. What God designed to meet our needs, Satan has converted into targets for our wants.

Utilizing the lust driven imaginations of men, the Deceiver has succeeded in assembling a collection of ideas, traditions, activities, and things which appeal to the very lusts and pride responsible for their formulation. The natural man loves the world because it mirrors his own fallen nature, and promises satisfaction to his cancerous appetites and selfish ambitions. The world encompasses all manner of principles, practices and things that meet the specifications of the lust of the flesh, the lust of the eyes, and the pride of life (I Jn 2:15-16). The world is the catalyst in the iniquity equation, the meeting place of Satan and man.

But won't the world at the end of the Millennium be different than it is today? Undoubtedly it will be. One thousand years of direct rule by its Creator, while Satan is imprisoned, couldn't help but filter out most of its vile practices and products, and improve its moral climate. However, despite this future improvement in the status of the world, Satan will still succeed in formulating a carrot that he can dangle before the sinful appetites of men; a blessing of God that he can distort into an attraction to covet after. Guess what it will be?

During the Millennium God will bless Israel both spiritually and physically beyond our highest expectations. Consider just one of His promises to them: "I will not turn away from doing them **good**...I will rejoice over doing them **good**, and I will plant them in the land in faithfulness with all my heart and will all my soul...so I will bring them all the **good** that I promised them"(Jer 32:40-42 MLB). God's goodness to Israel, and in particular the blessings bestowed upon the residents of Jerusalem, will be no secret. "All the nations will hear about all the good things which I do for them... the nations will tremble in awe at all the peace and prosperity that I provide for it (Jerusalem)" (Jer 33:9 NET). Though the entire earth of that day will benefit from the Lord's wise and righteous administration over them, foreign lands will not reap the same kind and degree of His blessings that Israel will. Some will likely even taste, when needed, the just correction of Him who will rule with a rod of iron, and consequently, may even harbor resentment against their international ruler.

When Satan, wearing his best disguise, makes his entrance into the last act of history, he will waste no time manipulating the stage setting of those sunset hours in a manner that will produce a modified world; one that includes a target compatible with the collective lusts of mankind. Utilizing lies, he will minimize the more than adequate wealth of the nations, and focus their attention on the immense riches of Israel. Utilizing the very jewel of God's blessing, he will place it in a worldly setting, transforming it into an object to be grasped after and stolen. It is interesting how the prize, which Satan will focus the attention of the nations upon, has changed hands. At one time, the Devil, appealing to Christ's humanity, offered him all

The Final Conflict

the riches of the world he then ruled; an offer Christ rejected. At the end of time, Satan will approach the Lord, not as a wealthy landowner, but as a pauper and a robber; attempting to steal back the treasure from which he has been dispossessed. Satan will utilize the wisdom that is from below to prepare for the nations a recipe that includes two of his favorite ingredients: **covetousness and jealousy.** The assets of Israel will be deceitfully incorporated into a lovely cake for the nations to covet after, a delicacy portrayed for their consumption. Before serving this treat, he will garnish it with a special frosting. A reminder of the favored status of Israel will be the topping designed to stimulate their jealousy. When this poisonous dessert is baked and served, we know what will happen; "For where jealousy and rivalry exist, there will be confusion and everything base" (Jas 3:15-16 MLB).

Is the foregoing scenario mere conjecture on my part? Will Satan actually transform the respect and amazement of the nations over God's goodness to Israel into a passion to acquire His benevolent prize for themselves? Yes, God's word states that Israel's wealth will be one of the motives for the final attack on the land. Gog and his hosts will say: "I will march against the land of villages,… I will seize booty and carry it away as plunder, assailing the (former) waste places now inhabited with people who were gathered from the nations, who have become possessed of cattle and goods and who dwell in the center of the earth" (Ezek 38:11-12 MLB). Note: Their target is the earth's bull's-eye.

Satan will actually take his final lie a step further. He will not only produce a target compatible with the lusts of men's flesh and eyes, but make a direct appeal to their pride of life as well. As has been historically true of many rulers on earth, the latter day kings will be characterized by a spirit of rebellion against their Creator. In fact, this common bond of animosity toward their Lord will be a key factor in uniting them. Satan, appealing to their pride, will lead them in a **plot directed against the Lord and against His Anointed One:** "**Let us** tear their restraining bands apart, and let us cast their shackles **from us** (Psa 2:2-3).

This declaration of independence (rebellion) echoes Satan's original battle cry, and expresses a popular principle of the world: "Stick up for your rights!" The Deceiver can make such a call for emancipation look as good and purposeful as the Gettysburg Address. This demand for separation may even constitute the battle cry that rings across the mountains of Israel when Gog and his hordes move south to encounter the One who rules with a rod of iron. Of course, they will already possess complete freedom to do what is right, their objective will be to remove His restraints against evil; to maneuver their sin nature around His roadblock of righteousness. Gog and his hordes will arrive at Jerusalem seeking not only an earthly prize, but an opportunity to flaunt their defiance of the God of heaven and earth.

Why will the nations gather for war at the end of time? For the very same reasons men initiate any war: All the partners in Mystery of Iniquity Incorporated will be present. The one formerly identified as the Anointed Cherub will meet with Espionage Agent #1, the flesh, in their favorite hangout, the world.

Factor A + Factor B + Factor C = Iniquity. There is no "right" combination of these elements, but when all three are present a strong and binding obsession can be produced in men. This allows Satan to have a strong hold on their hearts and minds. At the end of time he will exercise such control to completely deceive men and lead them to their mutual doom. It will be the last act in his puppet show, demonstrating both his evil, seductive powers and the depravity of the puppets. The mystery of iniquity will be exhibited for the final time.

Why will this post millennial event be the final war? Because **all the factors responsible for war will be vanquished.** That's something Christ is dedicated to accomplishing before He leaves his earthly throne for heaven.

In the preceding section of our study we already described the annihilation of the rebellious armies of the nations. In the Day of Judgment that will very shortly follow, all ungodly men are destroyed, i.e., eternally consigned to the Lake of Fire (Rev 20:11-15; II Pet 3:7). **FACTOR B is removed!**

We have reserved the announcement of one very important post-war development until this portion of our study. I'm sure you have already guessed what it is. Yes, it is common knowledge that the Devil, following the demise of his troops, will be thrown into the Lake of Burning Sulfur, where the Beast and the False Prophet will have already spent 1,000 years. There "they will be tormented day and night forever and ever" (Rev 20:10). **That takes care of FACTOR A!**

There is still further good news! Soon after the war concludes, the battlefield will disappear as this present earth passes away (Rev 21:1), melting in fervent heat (II Pet 3:7, 10). The polluted and contaminated world, the one in which Satan and mankind plotted their rebellions and produced their perversions, will be no more. **Scratch FACTOR C!** Gone will be the entire digestive system of lust and pride, as well as the dietician who designed its menus and prepared its meals. Even the dining room in which the Devil's delicacies have traditionally been offered will have disappeared.

Finally the stage is clear, a new heaven and a new earth is moved in, and **righteousness feels right at home**. That's a promise (II Pet 3:13). In the process of this renovation, a single last enemy is destroyed, one we will identify in the concluding paragraph of this study.

D. The Mystery Results In A Revelation

Let's now wind up our study of the Final Conflict by first considering a second question I inserted in my introductory remarks: Why would God choose to draw the curtain of history closed with a war? You might have considered some related questions: Why will He allow Satan a final opportunity to deceive mankind? Why won't He cast the Devil into the Eternal Lake of Fire at the same time as his illustrious emissaries the Beast and the False Prophet?

The best answer that I can come up with is that the personalities and events of that final hour represent a cast and scenes that are absolutely vital to God's script; they cannot be omitted or substituted for in his eternal drama. God, in His infinite wisdom, has installed them as essential components of His plan; **"A plan…to bring everything together in Christ, things in heaven and things on earth"** (Eph 1:10 MLB).

At this juncture in our pilgrimage, many of His acts and purposes remain somewhat obscure (I Cor 13:12); perhaps even unfathomable (Rom 11:33-34). Through the Holy Spirit (Jn 16:13; I Cor 2:10; I Jn 2:27), the Lord may choose to disclose more conclusive answers to us at a later date. Most frequently such enlightenment comes as we study His Word (Psa 119:130; Prov 2:3-6) and pray (Psa 119:18). We will not recognize some prophetic events until they are actually taking place before our very eyes (Jn 13:19; 14:29; 16:4). Many things we will not fully understand until He takes us to Himself (I Cor 13:12). Some things will very likely remain an eternal mystery–to us, but not to God (Deut 29:29). The important thing is that all His decisions and acts will sooner or later glorify Himself, i.e., they will be recognized as expressions of His holy attributes: His righteousness, His love, His grace, His wisdom, His power, etc.

The Lord has revealed to us at least one stated purpose for His Sovereign choice to allow this final war; a reason why He will permit, and even encourage, His enemies to invade Israel and surround Jerusalem.

In the 38th chapter of Ezekiel the Lord reveals a specific reason for the devastating punishment He will inflict upon Gog and His hordes as a result of their aggression. Immediately after describing the various waves of His righteous wrath which will sequentially crash down upon His enemies, the Lord makes this statement: **"Thus I will manifest my greatness and My holiness and make Myself known in the eyes of many nations: and they shall know that I am the Lord"** (vs. 23 MLB).

Where have we heard a similar statement by God earlier in our study? How about when we focused on, "the war of the Sovereign Lord's Great Day." At the conclusion of His great victory in that earlier confrontation with Satan's armies, the Lord announced: "Thus I will manifest My glory among the nations, and all **the nations shall see the judgments that I execute** and the hand that I have laid on them. From that

The Final Conflict

day onwards **the house of Israel shall know that I am the Lord their God**. And the nations shall know that the house of Israel went into captivity for their iniquity" (Ezek 39:21-23 MLB).

It appears that God has very similar purposes for each of the last two great conflicts, but do you distinguish any differences in His concluding statements for these two separate engagements? Did you notice that as a consequence of His victory at Armageddon God will provide revelations to both Israel and the gentile nations. However, the subject and scope of the things He will show them are quite different. To the nations He will vindicate His righteousness. To Israel, He will make himself personally known. He will unveil to the nations the righteousness He displayed in dealing with both Israel and themselves, but He will share His personal righteousness with the remnant of Israel; completely reversing their captivity, pouring out His Spirit upon them, and entering into a face-to-face, heart-to-heart relationship with them (Ezek 39:25-29).

During the final war, every Israelite will already know Christ intimately, and thus God has no further revelations for them at the conclusion of that war. However, most of the Gentiles do not share such a relationship with God at that future point in history. Thus God states that as a consequence of His victory in the final war, "**Many nations shall know that I am the Lord**." This is the very promise He had earlier made and faithfully kept with the Jews. If I correctly interpret God's Word to Ezekiel, some **survivors among the nations** will not merely recognize the absolute righteousness of God demonstrated in His final acts and judgments, but **they will come to personally know Him in a redeeming and transforming relationship.** His grace will reach out one final time to bring men into His eternal Kingdom at the midnight of history.

In the final act of all time, which we have been considering, all the major participants (the Lord, man, and Satan) gather to square off in an unfenced, peaceful arena, similar in several respects to the garden in which they met at the very dawn of time, age, and death. At the end of that critical but brief confrontation, Christ will be declared the overwhelming and eternal victor over Satan. This event will conclude a triumph first declared by God thousands of years in advance at Eden. Do you recall how the Lord God, addressing Satan then in the disguise of the serpent, not only pronounced his ultimate doom, but revealed the path through humanity and suffering that Christ Jesus would take to make His victory applicable to us: "And I will put enmity between you and the woman, between your offspring and hers; He will crush your head and you will strike His heel" (Gen 3:15).

In their final confrontation, Christ will deliver to Satan the blow that God, from the beginning of time, has guaranteed would terminate his influence. The Devil's ultimate doom has been even more predictable since the day Christ defeated him on the cross (Heb 2:14; Jn 12:31).

When Satan is consigned to the eternal Lake of Fire, the Lord still has one last enemy to defeat; not in war, but in resurrection. This final enemy was also first introduced to man at Eden. In the following text, which concludes our study, you will discover who this final enemy is. You will also note God's ultimate purpose for all His conquests. In addition, you will find, within this passage, an excellent reason why a war will terminate time; why this confrontation with Satan and rebellious mankind will be delayed until the very end of Christ's reign in Jerusalem.

> "**Then the end will come, when He hands over the Kingdom to God the Father after He (Christ) has destroyed all dominion, authority, and power. For He must reign until He has put all His enemies under His feet. The last enemy to be destroyed is death. For He 'has put everything under His feet.' Now when it says 'everything' has been put under Him, it is clear that this does not include God Himself, who put everything under Christ. When He has done this, then the Son will subject Himself to the One who put everything under Him SO THAT GOD MAY BE ALL IN ALL."**
> —I Cor 15:24-28

Pleasant Word

To order additional copies of this title:
Please visit our Web site at
www.pleasantwordbooks.com

If you enjoyed this quality custom-published book,
drop by our Web site for more books and information.

www.winepressgroup.com
"Your partner in custom publishing."